Golden Boats from Burma

THE LIFE OF ANN HASSELTINE JUDSON
THE FIRST AMERICAN WOMAN IN BURMA

by the author of

SARABAND FOR A SAINT
ME PAPOOSE SITTER
PRINCESS MARGARET
THE ENCHANTED BUNGALOW
THE GYPSY CONDESA
PETER JUMPING HORSE
PETER JUMPING HORSE AT THE RODEO

GOLDEN
BOATS
FROM
BURMA

by Gordon Langley Hall

MACRAE SMITH COMPANY: PHILADELPHIA

for

HASSELTINE WHITNEY
whose memory still lingers sweetly
in the old house
where this book was written

and

my great-aunt

SARAH KATE ASHDOWN
who for ninety years
has been a tower of strength
to the Baptist cause

By this my gift, whatever boon I seek,
It is the best of boons to profit all;
By this abundant merit I desire
Here or hereafter no angelic pomp
Of Brahmas, Suras, Maras; nor the state
And splendors of a monarch; nay, not even
To be the pupil of a conqueror.
But I would build a causeway sheer athwart
The river of Samsara, and all folk
Would speed across thereby until they reach
The Blessed City. I myself would cross,
And drag the drowning over. Aye, myself
Tamed, I would tame the willful; comforted,
Comfort the timid; wakened, wake the asleep;
Cool, cool the burning; freed, set free the bound.

King Alaungsithu of Burma.
(1112—1167).

Golden Boats from Burma

THE LIFE OF ANN HASSELTINE JUDSON
THE FIRST AMERICAN WOMAN IN BURMA

prologue

The wounded British officer crouched on the shore anxiously watching the quiet waters of the Irrawaddy River for sign of a friendly craft. He had almost lost count of time since the Burmese boatmen who manned his canoe had suddenly attacked him. They had fought and overpowered him, taken his possessions and left him for dead on the shore.

Night cast a mystical spell over the lush foilage that grew down to the river's edge. A slight breeze rippled through the mango trees and there was a sickly odor of wild date palms close to the steaming water.

The mosquitoes were already troublesome. At frequent intervals when disturbed at their slumber monkeys and birds set up a jarring chatter.

Then the moon came out and he saw the procession of

golden boats. At first he did not know if they were friend or foe. Better to be taken a prisoner by the enemy with the chance of possible ransom than be left to one's fate at the edge of the jungle. He shouted "Help!" at the top of his lungs.

After what seemed an eternity he realized that the occupants in the first of the small flotilla had seen him. A skiff was being dispatched to his rescue.

A few minutes later his wounds were being dressed by a young woman with soft brown eyes. The British officer did not realize that he was looking at Ann Hasseltine Judson, the first American woman ever to set foot in the fabled land of Burma, but he could never forget the obvious devotion of the man and woman who were helping him. Tired and worn though they appeared, their very movements seemed to act in quiet unison, he tearing what looked to be an old shirt into strips of bandage, she methodically taking them to dress their unexpected patient's wounds.

The year 1826 was a time of trouble for the Golden Presence, the fabulous King of Burma, and his people. For some time the country had been invaded by the British under the command of Sir Archibald Campbell who, in return for peace, had demanded a crore of rupees equal to the vast sum of a million British pounds sterling. In return Sir Archibald had promised that with the exception of the coastal provinces the country would be left to the Burmese. The long golden boat that had rescued the wounded officer was carrying part of the first instalment.

At Ava, City of the Golden Fleet, the King had reluctantly given orders for the pile of silver bars to be carried to the waiting boats. Beautiful vases and other works of art were being melted down to provide more.

Ann, her missionary husband, Adoniram Judson, and their

baby daughter Maria had been allowed to leave Ava along with the silver. They had been in Burma for thirteen years. Adoniram had only recently been released from the dreaded Let-may-yoon Prison. His wife was barely recovered from a near-fatal attack of spotted fever.

To the young missionaries, as to the wounded British officer, the slow voyage down the Irrawaddy River was like a real taste of heaven. *They were free.*

Pale and gaunt, her black hair close-cropped as part of her recent fever treatment, Ann looked only the ghost of the young girl who had exchanged the quiet home of her forefathers in Bradford, Massachusetts, for a life of adventure in the Orient. She sat close to her husband, a man prematurely aged by suffering and privation. At their feet lay the baby Maria, her little arms and legs so thin for lack of nourishment that they looked like sticks. The officer would have much to tell his comrades when they reached the British camp at Yandabo.

Fascinated, Ann gazed towards the moonlit shoreline. Screwpines, ironwood, banana trees . . . She easily recognised the dark outlines of some of the shrubbery. Now they were passing a primitive settlement of bamboo dwellings built out from the river bank and hanging perilously over the water. She guessed they belonged to fishermen, for there were nets hung across rough frames to dry. Beneath a group of banyan trees for an instant she glimpsed the sleek orange back of a tiger.

Dawn broke at last over the river. Pale streamers of pink and mauve streaked across the gray-blue sky.

"Look, a steamboat. It must be the *Diana*." Ann's husband broke the silence, his voice full of excitement.

"Where, Don?" Her eyes were still heavy from lack of sleep. Then she, too, saw the masts of the *Diana*, that magical vessel that had impressed the Burmese so much, making them believe the British invincible. Shortly afterwards she and the baby were taken aboard the steamboat.

Adoniram, accompanied by the young officer they had rescued, continued a few miles farther downstream with the treasure boats to Sir Archibald's camp at Yandabo, and returned later that night with the pleasant news that the British commander had invited them to come and stay at his camp.

They left next day, and on their arrival at Yandabo Sir Archibald sent his own son to escort Ann from the steamboat. Her arrival caused a tremendous boost in the morale of the British soldiers, who christened her the Heroine of Ava. Whenever she made an appearance on the verandah attached to her tent, she was spontaneously greeted with cheering. The British were determined to treat her like visiting royalty. She dined with her husband at Sir Archibald's own table and often remarked to Adoniram that he was treating them both "with the kindness of a father." In a letter home to New England she wrote, "No persons on earth were ever happier than we were during the fortnight we passed at the English camp."

Ann had her greatest triumph at the state dinner given by Sir Archibald for the Burmese commissioners with whom he had been negotiating what history knows as the Treaty of Yandabo.

The British Commander well knew the love of the Burmese for color and pomp. He was determined to impress them. Flags and banners turned the camp into a wonderland. Hangings of gold, red and yellow bunting welcomed the rather uneasy guests.

A long dinner table had been set up. Even a regimental band was provided. Sir Archibald, wearing a splendid uni-

14

form, himself led the grand procession. His officers, along with the reluctant Burmese commissioners, formed themselves in couples to follow. The band struck up a stirring march; the Burmese were suitably impressed, their eyes watching Sir Archibald's every movement. As the procession reached the Judson tent the British commander called, "Halt!" Alone he entered the tent, reappearing shortly afterwards with Mrs. Judson on his arm.

Poised and smiling, Ann accompanied him in to dinner where she was given the place of honor at his right hand.

The Burmese Commissioners looked even more uncomfortable. All but one of them had witnessed the miserable treatment Ann had suffered during the past few months while her husband was in prison. They had seen her begging for food in the streets; had known of her grim illness. One of them in particular had even more to fear from her vengeance than the others—for they were certain Ann would demand retribution for the merciless way some had treated her.

Sir Archibald noticed the worried faces of the commissioners. He saw them mop the perspiration from their brows and pass aside the splendid courses of food. "I fancy these gentlemen must be old acquaintances of yours," he said, touching Ann lightly on the arm. "Judging from their appearance you must have treated them very badly."

For once she could not control her natural sense of humor. The Hasseltine laughter of old rippled through the cool night air.

The Burmese commissioner who most feared Ann shook from head to foot. The food slipped from his fork. His behavior attracted Sir Archibald's eye.

"What is the matter with the owner of the pointed beard

over there?" he inquired of Ann. "He seems to be seized with a fit of ague."

Ann smiled. "I do not know," she replied, "unless his memory may be too busy. He is an old acquaintance of mine. Probably he considers himself in danger now that he sees me under your protection."

Then she told the British general her story, of how one day, still suffering from fever, she had walked through stifling streets to this particular commissioner's house to beg help for her husband who, pinioned with five pairs of fetters, had been thrown into prison. She had hoped by traveling early in the morning to escape the heat but the commissioner made her wait outside his door until noon before granting an audience. He hardly listened to her pleas for help, being more interested in the silk umbrella she carried as a shield against the burning sun. When she finished speaking he snatched it from her hand like a petulant child. She begged him, if he kept the silk umbrella, at least in return to give her a paper one. With a mocking laugh he shouted, "Only fat people need to fear sunstroke. The sun can't find a woman as thin as you."

Although he did not understand English, the guilty commissioner knew he was under discussion. He could not fail to see the looks of anger on the faces of the British officers. He was sure that he would be executed.

Then Ann noticed the color of his face. He was still shaking. Enough was enough; he had had his punishment. Softly she said in Burmese, "You have nothing to fear."

She had crossed wide oceans to reach this strange, exciting land of Burma. The years had been hard, yet she would not have exchanged her life with Adoniram for any other. When the British demanded that all foreigners

16

be allowed to leave the country, it was the Golden Presence himself who decreed that all but Adoniram, little Maria and herself might go.

"They are not English," he had insisted. "They are my people. They shall not go."

His people. Ann smiled. She fingered lovingly the silken folds of her Burmese robe. Somewhere in the far distance a woman was singing:

> *"This chickrassia which I planted,*
> *Isn't it lovely? Tiny buds on slender stems.*
> *But if you pluck them before they flower,*
> *My plant will wither away, you know."*

one

JUNE 27, 1810.

BRADFORD,

MASSACHUSETTS

"Ann, I hope one day you will be satisfied with rambling." Rebecca Burton Hasseltine spoke from her seat in the spacious bay window of the tall white frame house that stood looking northward toward the blue waters of the Merrimack River. Mrs. Hasseltine, whose face still bore traces of great beauty, closed her book and beckoned her youngest daughter to sit beside her.

Ann placed the bouquet of bittersweet and lady's slipper in her mother's lap. "These will help brighten up the room for tomorrow."

Mrs. Hasseltine nodded. She looked closely at Ann's smiling face, at the jet-black curls and delicate white hands. Ann was a charmer, there was no doubt of that. She was

19

her father's favorite child and had meant more to him since their son John had been lost at sea a year before. Even when, at sixteen, Ann forgot that she was a young lady and was caught chasing thirteen-year-old Rufus Anderson with a stick, her father couldn't punish her.

Deacon John Hasseltine had more than once said of his daughter, "Where she is, no one can be gloomy or unhappy." Mrs. Hasseltine agreed that generally this was the case, although of late Ann had worried her a little. The girl often spent long, unexplained hours alone in her room and she seemed restless and uneasy. Her father believed that Salem had something to do with it.

Ann had been teaching school in Salem, boarding with her friend Lydia Kimball whose family had a store on Essex Street full of merchandise advertised as "European and India goods." Ann and Lydia often visited the store and there was nothing quite so thrilling as the red-letter days when bales of gaily colored silks and satins arrived from the far-off East.

Just to be staying in Salem was exciting, especially to a girl with a vivid imagination. The houses were richer and finer than those in Ann's native Bradford. The great ship-owners had built for themselves luxurious homes with elaborately carved mantels and overmantels designed by Samuel McIntire, their leading architect and skilful wood-carver, whose beautiful work was to the New Englanders what Grinling Gibbons' had been in the mother country.

Ann never tired of listening to the fabulous tales of adventure told by the bearded sea captains. With Lydia she often visited the wharfs on Derby Street to watch the clipper ships unload their precious cargoes. Breathlessly the girls would watch as these same ships, their unfurled sails billowing in the breeze, started off on their voyages toward far, romantic horizons.

There were other times when Ann, craving silence to dream, would steal out on her own without Lydia. Always the water seemed to beckon her and, with the taste of salt on her lips, she would sigh with envy as the graceful vessels edged out to sea by Baker's Island and Big and Little Misery. "I'll never be content to stay home all my life in Essex County," was the disturbing thought that recurred over and over in her mind. She knew that the spirit of adventure lying unfulfilled in her mother had been passed on to her. Her brother John had had the same urge to wander—an urge that had led him early to a watery grave. Yet she believed that, short as her brother's life was, it had been a full one. From the time he was a small boy he had longed to go to sea, and in the end the sea had claimed him. At least he had achieved his desire—because he was a man. Properly brought up young ladies, Ann knew, simply did not serve before the mast. Instead they stayed at home where, if they were bright, they could take up teaching as a career and with good luck even marry a clergyman, as her sister Rebecca had done.

Each day spent in bustling Salem only made Ann the more restless and anxious as to what the future might hold.

Though unpretentious, the Hasseltine home in Bradford was ample and comfortable for the needs of Deacon and Mrs. Hasseltine and their three daughters Abigail, Mary and —before her marriage—Rebecca, named for her mother. The large, low-beamed kitchen with the delicious smell of baked bread coming from the deep brick oven was the most lived-in room of the house. The parlor's bay window had been built for Mrs. Hasseltine's special use. There on sunny days she could sit and read. Rebecca Hasseltine read more books in a month than most Bradford women did in a year! The walls of the parlor were pleasantly stenciled with wedding bells and bows; the floor was painted a reddish brown. Rebecca and her daughters themselves had made the hooked rugs during the long winter evenings.

On one side of the room stood the best mahogany sideboard with the silver candlesticks that had belonged to her grandmother. Displayed on the open shelves were some handleless cups, saucers and plates made of the fashionable grayish-white Export porcelain brought on the clipper ships all the way from China. John had given the set to his mother just before he went to sea.

Ann saw her mother looking at the sideboard and guessed what she was thinking. Going over, she picked up one of the delicate, cool-feeling plates and examined the golden sun-ray design in the center with the outer ring of tiny blue dots arranged like flowers.

"I'm sure these are meant to be forget-me-nots," she said, and her mother smiled. She rose to her feet.

"Come, Ann, let's put your flowers in water and then I'll show you the pies I have baked for tomorrow."

Tomorrow. Ann was looking forward to it with more excitement than she cared to admit. A certain young man of twenty-two, named Adoniram Judson, was coming to dine with them. That he was no ordinary young man she was sure, for he had recently turned down the associate ministry of one of Boston's most famous churches because he had some high-minded notion to be a missionary.

All the town was talking of how young Judson planned a ten-mile walk to their meeting house with three companions to request that they be sent by the churches of Massachusetts as the first American missionaries to the Far East.

All the families in Bradford and nearby Haverhill wanted

to meet Mr. Judson but it was at the Hasseltine house, Ann noted with some satisfaction, that he had chosen to dine.

In the morning she would help her mother lay the long table in the pleasant west room. Unconsciously she fingered the post of one of the doors. How solid and strong it stood. She was grateful for this home that had sheltered her so long, and for her parents. Surely she had the most unusual parents in the whole of New England. Her father liked nothing more than to see the young people happy. He had even added a large room on the second floor of their house to be used as a "frolics room" where his children could entertain their friends, play games and dance. With tongue in cheek Deacon Hasseltine dismissed the murmurings of some of his more Puritan-minded neighbors who sarcastically dubbed the frolics room the Hasseltine Dance Hall. He was used to criticism, as was his literary-minded wife. For one thing they believed in the higher education of women, a rather touchy subject in those days. They had carried out these alarming theories by having their daughters educated just as carefully as their son.

two

Ann was standing in front of the broad window sill of the west room in the Hasseltine home when he first saw her. For Adoniram Judson it was love at first sight.

Only that morning he had heard the local story of how Ann had been responsible for the "conversion" of her father. At the age of fifteen she had come under the influence of Abraham Burnham, the newly appointed preceptor of Bradford Academy. Burnham, whose father was a farmer at Dunbarton, New Hampshire, had come about his own education through great personal sacrifice. To raise the money for his ministerial studies he had taken the scholastic position at Bradford and during the vacation periods he earned extra sums by teaching in Concord, New Hampshire. He considered it his duty to guide the young people entrusted to his care into a religious way of life. Happy-go-lucky Ann Hasseltine, who at fourteen years had given up saying her prayers when she returned home rather tired from parties "thinking, that as I was old enough to attend balls, I was surely too old to say prayers" was one of the first to be affected by Burnham's dynamic personality. One Sunday morning she was all dressed for church when her eyes caught sight of the much-read book *Strictures on Female Education* by Hannah More. For some reason feeling impelled to open it, she was confronted by the startling sentence "She that liveth in pleasure, is dead while she liveth."

Not wishing to upset herself on such a beautiful morning, she put down the offending book; yet, try as she would in the days that followed, she could not forget the warning it contained. A few months later, for a "Sabbath book," she began to read John Bunyan's *Pilgrim's Progress*. She noted that "Christian, because he adhered to the narrow path, was carried safely through all his trials, and at last admitted into heaven."

After that Ann searched her soul for guidance in leading a suitable religious life, coming to the conclusion that the quickest way to be saved was to stay home instead of attending parties, "and be reserved and serious in the presence of other scholars."

However it was not easy for a girl whose second nature was to be gay. Next day when asked to a party she did in fact refuse, but upon being asked to another she succumbed and accepted, excusing herself on the grounds that it was really only a family gathering. When the fiddles struck up the first dance Ann Hasseltine joined in the festivities. She was the life of the party that evening and in her own words "thought no more of the new life I had just begun."

But Ann's conscience bothered her. It was Abraham Burnham who eventually solved her dilemma. He loved to visit the Hasseltine home with its marriageable daughters, for he was still unwed at thirty. One evening he told the company that the Devil tempted people "to conceal their true feelings from others lest their religious convictions should increase."

The remark echoed in Ann's heart so that she felt herself to be the Devil's prisoner, not having the courage to tell her more frivolous friends of her religious convictions. A visit to an understanding aunt helped the confused girl, after which she found comfort spending much of her spare time quietly praying in her room.

One night her genial, good-natured father who had no patience with what he called "experimental piety" was coming in from the fields when, passing a window, he saw Ann on her knees with her head bowed in prayer. The sight made him stop short; then, turning abruptly, he hurried off in the direction of a favorite oak tree. On reaching it, he threw himself upon the ground and in a voice punctuated with great sobs poured out his heart to his Maker.

This was the story that Adoniram had heard, and he liked it. Apart from Ann's beauty, he found himself thinking what excellent material she would make for a pioneer missionary's wife!

Ann too was watching Adoniram as she cut a deep-dish chicken pie into man-size portions. Frankly she was a little disappointed. He was smaller than she had imagined and his nose seemed rather prominent. The curly chestnut hair with which the Lord had so liberally endowed him was by far Adoniram's best feature.

The Reverend Jonathan Allen, or Parson Allen as he

was familiarly known, pastor of Bradford's First Church, decided that it was high time for Ann and Adoniram to be introduced.

Ann paused long enough in her pie cutting to shake hands with the young man who was so determined to be a missionary. If she had expected Adoniram to say something particularly bright, witty or intelligent, three virtues in which she had been told he excelled, she was doomed to disappointment. The young man was practically speechless. What was more, he left most of his dinner.

She mentioned this fact to her mother, who decided that Adoniram was probably thinking of the speech he had to make at the meeting that afternoon. On the contrary, Adoniram Judson's head was filled with thoughts of the girl with the pie.

That evening Ann listened carefully as her father described the impression young Mr. Judson had made on the distinguished delegates gathered for the afternoon session in the First Church, which stood on the green near Kimball Tavern.

The daring missionary undertaking that at first had sounded "wild and romantic" to the solemn-faced ministers, to say nothing of the general public who filled the gallery, had actually been approved. Adoniram's short speech, coupled with his own determination, was a resounding success.

After the delegates had departed for their various homes Bradford settled back into its old quiet ways. All but Ann Hasseltine. If she had been restless after her visit to bustling Salem she was now more so than ever. She took long walks by the quick-flowing waters of the Merrimack River which the Indians had so aptly called "the place of strong currents." The meadows were ablaze with buttercups and white daisies; the air was sweet with the scent of honeysuckle. Sometimes she took a path through the woods beneath the lacelike branches of tall wineglass elms that towered high over maple, hemlock, shagbark and pine.

This was the age of religious revival in America; Ann longed to do something really useful with her life. More than once her mind strayed to the young minister. Somehow she could not put him out of her mind. Then one afternoon the stagecoach brought her a letter from Adoniram Judson.

Impulsively Ann broke the wax seal, read a few lines and gasped. "Of all the arrogant . . ." She got no further, for her mother had come into the room. Anne marched out into the garden, leaving the offending letter on the parlor table.

Everybody in the Hasseltine household became aware of Adoniram's proposal; Ann took care that they should. She had always been the pet of the family and was used to sharing problems. Her sister Rebecca had recently married a clergyman; Abigail was teaching at Beverly. Only Mary was home.

For a month Ann did nothing to set her suitor's mind at rest. At last Mary asked, "Have you answered that letter of Mr. Judson's?"

"No," Ann replied.

"Then if you don't, I shall," threatened her elder sister.

"Maybe Ann is disturbed by so long a name as Adoniram," teased their mother. "You know the original Adoniram supervised the tribute in Solomon's treasury."

"She can shorten it to Don," retorted the practical Mary. Adoniram or Don, Ann Hasseltine wrote him a letter that evening, in which she said neither Yes nor No. She informed him that in any case her parents would have to give their consent.

If this was meant to discourage the ardent Adoniram, it had the exactly opposite effect. At once he wrote to Ann's father. The contents so upset one of Deacon Hasseltine's friends that he vowed that he would tie his own daughter to her fourposter bed rather then let her loose on such a harebrained escapade.

In the sonorous language of his calling Adoniram declared,

I have now to ask, whether you can consent to part with your daughter early next spring, to see her no more in this world; whether you can consent to her departure, and her subjection to the hardships and sufferings of a missionary life; whether you can consent to her exposure to the dangers of the ocean; to the fatal influence of the southern climate of India; to every kind of want and distress; to degradation, insult, persecution, and perhaps a violent death.

Deacon Hasseltine had already lost one child to the ocean; now he was being asked to part with the favorite of the family with only the remotest chance of ever seeing her again. Ann would not be twenty-one until December 22.

Her mother wished she would not leave them but thought the girl should make her own decision. Secretly she had always believed this youngest daughter was destined to travel. In a way she even envied her; Rebecca Hasseltine's own wanderings were only of the armchair kind.

To the credit of the deacon, who was faced with a barrage of criticism from well-meaning neighbors, he stoutly declared, "Whatever her choice she must make up her own mind. Then she will have my blessing."

"It's utterly improper," sniffed one Bradford matron who

had ventured her unasked opinion on his daughter's proposed alliance and life with the would-be missionary.

"It is altogether preposterous for a woman to consider such a rash undertaking," declared another from within the safe depths of her large purple bonnet.

Don—as she was already calling him—was now a regular visitor to the Hasseltine home. Under the low covered bridge he would walk with Ann on his arm. Then at other times they would gallop their horses through the green fields surrounding the Hasseltine home, for they were both excellent riders. Rebecca, Ann's mother, would watch from her own special bay window as the handsome young couple returned from such an adventure, their faces flushed with good health and excitement. There was no mistaking the way Ann looked at young Mr. Judson.

As for Adoniram, Ann knew now that he really loved her. Unpredictable though he might be, she had come to realize that when he made up his mind to do something there was no shaking him from his avowed purpose. At their first brief meeting he had decided that she was the woman with whom he wished to share his life's work, and as the long summer sped by she found herself coming more and more under the spell of his vital personality. Each day she found her desire to share his hopes and dreams grow stronger. She felt too that he was going to need her.

Bold, with the courage of his convictions, Adoniram needed a tactful wife who could cope with any emergency. Above everything else, a missionary's wife would need her full share of common sense.

Mary Hasseltine was in later life to recall Adoniram as he appeared when he first came calling as her sister's suitor, "in the ardor of his first love. It may literally be said that he was a man of one idea, and that was, love, to Jesus, and a desire to manifest it in all its varied forms. Yet he was by nature ardent, impetuous, and ambitious, with the most unshaken confidence in his own judgment, irrespective of the advice of his elders."

Tongue-in-cheek, Adoniram, in his firm round handwriting, wrote Samuel Nott, another destined for the mission field, "I have done nothing scarcely since I saw you, beside making a compilation of extracts for the Collection of Letters attending to this missionary business and riding about the country with Ann. [He had scratched out the word 'Nancy'—her pet-name.] Pretty preparation this last article, for a missionary life—isn't it?"

Ann soon learned that Adoniram's dream was to serve, not in India, but as the first American missionary to the fabled land of Burma. On one of his frequent visits he left her a copy of *An Account of An Embassy to the Kingdom of Ava*. It was written by a British Army officer named Michael Symes who in 1795 had been sent by the Governor-General of India to Ava, capital of the Burmese Empire.

One afternoon she took the book to discuss it with her close friend, Harriet Atwood, who was not quite seventeen. Harriet lived with her widowed mother over the river in Haverhill. She was not a strong girl. Only two years before, her father had died of what was then the dread disease of tuberculosis. Although deeply religious, she was astounded by Ann's decision to quit her native America and serve their God in far-off Asia.

She adored Ann Hasseltine in a way that almost amounted to heroine worship. Of a somewhat quieter disposition herself, she was proud to be singled out as the best friend of the most popular of the Hasseltine sisters.

Fascinated, Harriet listened carefully as Ann read aloud from Michael Symes' book:

"There are no countries on the habitable globe, where the arts of civilized life are understood, of which we have so limited a knowledge, as those that lie between the British possessions in India and the empire of Burma."

Ann went on to tell of the Golden King who lived in the golden city of Ava. Everything about him was referred to as golden. To pay him homage was to kneel at the Golden Feet; when news was brought him it "reached the Golden Ears." Although an absolute monarch, he had no ambitions to conquer the rest of the world, for he thought it hardly worth the trouble. His land was filled with fabulous temples honoring the Buddha, and of these there were five thousand in the ancient royal city of Pagan alone. Many of their interiors were decorated with brilliant mosaics, made from tiny pieces of glass, depicting processions of elephants and horses, courtiers and priests. Most famed of all the temples was the Shwe-dagon Pagoda whose golden dome towered over the busy seaport of Rangoon.

Harriet sat entranced as her friend continued to read descriptions of noblemen in flowing robes of silk, velvet and satin, with their velvet caps covered with flowers of gold. From their ears hung trumpet-shaped rings that were at least three inches long.

Golden war-vessels with cannons at the bow were rowed into battle by more than fifty oarsmen singing victory songs. Some of these strange, narrow craft measured a hundred feet from prow to stern.

Then Ann told of the riches of Burma, of the great teak

forests coveted by the British for shipbuilding, of natural wells oozing with a crude oil which scientists called petroleum. The Burmese collected this evil-smelling liquid to use in their lamps. Officer Symes was not very interested, for not once did he trouble to visit these wells. Gold, silver, rubies, amethysts, sapphires, garnets, amber and jasper were to be mined in profusion.

To the two New England girls reading together on that quiet afternoon in Haverhill the vivid description sounded more like the contents of Solomon's fabulous temple.

Little did Ann Hasseltine think as she returned home to supper that she had done more than just entertain the frail Harriet Atwood. In less than a month from Harriet's meeting with Ann another young missionary volunteer, Samuel Newell, had entered the former's life, which prompted Adoniram to comment in a letter that "Brother Newell is preaching and residing at West Haverhill. Matrimonial matters in train." Harriet too was destined for distant exotic shores.

three

One by one the flaming maple leaves fell to the ground, the earth turned to stone and the first snowflakes drifted over the New England countryside.

In January 1811, Adoniram sailed on the *Packet,* a British vessel outward bound from Boston Harbor to England. It was a perilous time to be sailing the high seas. Britain and France were at war, while the United States stood on the brink of hostilities with both of them.

It was hard for Ann to see him go. The dangers of such a journey were great and the voyage to England would take two months at least. The mails were slow and Ann would miss Adoniram's letters, for in the last few weeks they had become an important part of her existence. Never could anybody accuse him of having writer's cramp. When, because of his preparations for sailing to England, he could not see her, he would send a love letter in which he poured out his heart. They were amazing letters for a young man in love, but then Adoniram was an amazing young man. On New Year's morning, while suffering from a nasty cold, he wrote her,

It is with the utmost sincerity, and with my whole heart, that I wish you, my love, a happy new year. May it be a year in which your walk will be close with God; your frame calm and serene; and the road that leads you to the Lamb marked with purer light. May it be a year in which you will have more largely the spirit of Christ, be praised above sublunary things, and be willing to be disposed of in this world just as God shall please. As every moment of the year will bring you nearer to the end of your pilgrimage, may it bring you nearer to God, and find you more prepared to hail the messenger of death as a deliverer and friend. And now, since I have begun to wish, I will go on. May this be the year in which you change your name; in which you take final leave of your relatives and native land; in which you will cross the wide ocean, and dwell on the other side of the world, among a heathen people."

It seemed to Ann that she was just beginning to understand the impulsive young man who always thought he was right, usually ending up by getting his own way. Still it was essential for what the neighbors still called the "wild romantic undertaking" that he should make the long journey to London on behalf of the Commissioners of the newly-formed American (Missionary) Board to see if some joint combination might be made with the experienced London Missionary Society. Adoniram was to sound out the possibility of the London Society's providing funds, or at least most of them, for the maintenance of the first American missionaries to Asia.

The voyage turned into a nightmare for Adoniram when his ship was attacked by a French privateer sailing under the formidable name, *L'Invincible Napoléon*. The *Packet* fell an easy victim. Adoniram, together with two rich Spanish merchants, the officers and crew, was taken prisoner.

It was all right for the merchants, the only other passengers. Able to speak French, they were well treated, given good quarters and a place at the captain's table. Dressed in his somber clerical clothes, Adoniram did not fare as well. Nobody seemed to realize he was a minister and so he found himself thrown into the Frenchman's hold along with the crew.

As Ann was later to discover, Adoniram's dislike for any kind of dirt amounted almost to an obsession. His first taste of what he might find as a missionary came in the filthy, vermin-ridden hold of *L'Invincible Napoléon*. Dirty, disheveled, homesick and seasick, he began to have second thoughts as to whether he had chosen the right vocation for Ann and himself. Pictures of the trim Boston church he had rejected passed frequently through his mind. Doubts assailed him on every side, until finally he began to wonder if God were not testing his powers of endurance.

The hold seemed to pitch more than ever in the rough wintry sea; men were being sick all around him. Summoning up his strength, he managed to get to his knees. Then he prayed for strength. His prayers were answered, and feeling a little better, he groped in the darkness for his Hebrew Bible. At last it was in his hand. Slowly he faltered toward a dim stream of daylight that leaked into the darkness. He kept his mind busy translating, word by word, the Hebrew text into Latin.

A few days later the ship's doctor chanced to hear him translating aloud. Understanding Latin, he found it a method of communication with the young American, and much surprised, eventually discovered his calling. Overjoyed, Adoniram exchanged the stench-laden hold for a berth in one of the cabins. He was allowed to join the ship's officers and the two rich Spanish merchants when the captain dined.

Before docking at Bayonne, the French privateer first landed the merchants at Le Passage, Spain. At Bayonne Adoniram was treated once more as a prisoner, being taken at gunpoint, along with the *Packet's* crew, to be locked in the local jail. If a friendly American from Philadelphia had not spotted him as a fellow countryman, how long Adoniram would have been imprisoned is a matter for conjecture. Rescued by the Philadelphian, who had bribed the guards, Adoniram did not reach his destination in England until May, having left Boston just four months before. In June, his assignment completed, he sailed on the *Augustus* for home and a much-anticipated reunion with Ann.

Once more the elders of the church (now known as the officials of the American Board) gathered to hear Adoniram Judson, this time in Worcester, Massachusetts. The leaders of the London Missionary Society were not in favor of a joint enterprise. They were quite willing, however, to employ Adoniram and the other American missionary volunteers in their own service and to accept some American funds, but— they stated it emphatically—the direction of the enterprise had to remain in British hands.

Many of the elders were apathetic. Adoniram, determined and outspoken as usual, declared in a loud voice, "If you will not send me, I will become a missionary of the English organization."

They were on the brink of war; delaying a decision might well mean the American missionary volunteers would be kept from sailing to Asia for years. On this occasion Adoniram's impetuous outburst acted as an ultimatum. If the American society refused to send him he would go anyway. This "take it or leave it" attitude had the desired effect on the troubled elders, who voted to appoint Adoniram Judson, Samuel Newell, Gordon Hall and Samuel Nott, Jr., as missionaries "to labor under the direction of the board in Asia."

Adoniram's salary would be $666.66 a year as a married man, together with a further sum equal to a year's salary for outfitting. Three hundred dollars were allotted with which all the missionaries were to buy books.

Adoniram was jubilant. As usual he had got what he wanted. Now more money must be raised, a ship found and, most important of all, the date set for his wedding to the patient Miss Hasseltine.

While Adoniram had been in Europe Ann had been eagerly following the course of another romance—one in which she herself had played no small part. Just two days after she had told her friend Harriet Atwood that she was going to marry Adoniram, Samuel Newell had been introduced into the Atwood home by an acquaintance of the family. Shy and retiring, he had immediately been attracted to the frail quiet Harriet.

Ann, knowing that Newell expected to accompany Adoniram and herself on their perilous adventure to the Far East, could hardly be blamed for hoping that Harriet's friendship for the young man would develop into love. In any case Harriet was her closest friend, and how much less lonely would the missionary adventure be if another woman were included!

At times Ann wished that she could give Samuel Newell a push in the right direction, for he was so long in plucking up courage to send that all-important letter of proposal to Harriet. Compared with impatient Adoniram, Samuel was very slow indeed. Doubtless Harriet thought the same thing.

Six months passed before Samuel finally wrote Harriet of his intentions. Actually his hesitation was only due to the precarious state of Harriet's health. His attachment to her had swiftly grown into love but he was forced to admit that the terrible hardships of a pioneer missionary's life might prove too much of a strain for the sickly girl. Then one day a mutual friend remarked that "a little slender woman may endure losses and suffering as cheerfully and resolutely as an apostle." This was just the extra incentive he needed. Besides, Ann would be there to help Harriet over the roughest ground. Surely this, combined with his own devotion, would see her through.

Harriet, her heart beating heavily, broke the red seal on Samuel's letter and hurriedly began to read. Later she wrote:

I broke the seal, and what were my emotions, when I read the name of ———. This was not a long-wished-for letter, —no, it was a long-dreaded one, which, I was conscious, would involve me in doubts, anxiety, and distress. Nor were the contents such as I might answer at a distant period; they required an *immediate* answer. And now what shall I say? How shall I decide this *important*, this *interesting* ques-

40

tion? Shall I consent to leave forever the *Parent* of my youth; the *friends* of my life; the dear scenes of my childhood, and my native country; and go to a land of strangers, 'not knowing the things that shall befal me there'?

Harriet's mother, like the Hasseltine parents, announced that she had left to her daughter the important decision as to whether or not to marry a missionary. She told Harriet, "If a conviction of duty, and love to the souls of the perishing heathen, lead you to India, as much as I love you, Harriet, I can only say *Go*." Harriet accepted Samuel Newell's proposal.

It was fall again, the fall of 1811. During their walks along the Merrimack both Adoniram and Ann were saddened by the thought that this might be the last New England autumn they would ever see. The long narrow leaves of the chestnuts were turning to dusky brown; the wineglass elms, a delicate yellow. Bronze, golden and fiery red were the maples. Little wonder that the two young people, both prone by character towards the dramatic, were caught up in the majestic grandeur of it all. Unlike most travelers about to depart on a journey, they planned *never to return*. The journey to Burma would be one way only.

Fall merged into winter, the first rains fell and the trees were bare. Then came the snow, and still there was no news of a ship. Everybody believed war with England to be imminent. "A SHIP HAS TO BE FOUND," Adoniram told Ann. There were other worries too, financial ones. The committee of the American Board had only five hundred dollars in hand. With Britain and the United States actually at war, communications with the Far East would be few. The missionaries might be stranded for years without means of support. It all seemed a very tricky enterprise. Then, when difficulties were at their worst, news came of a ship sailing from Salem to Calcutta. A certain Pickering Dodge had received assurance from the United States government that his brig *Caravan* could sail on February 10. Besides her cargo she could take three or four passengers.

The old seafaring town of Salem had seen many sailings but never one quite like this. Across New England the word spread that two young men, New Englanders at that, Adoniram Judson and Samuel Newell, were sailing on a journey of no return. Were they martyrs or crazy? Most of all, their brides would go with them; that pleasant, jolly Miss Hasseltine who could not be more than twenty-one, to say nothing of fragile little Harriet Atwood. What would her late father have said? Besides, she was not yet seventeen.

As the news spread, so did the money come in from generous people caught up in the religious fervor and adventure of it all. No longer was the wild Burmese undertaking a pipe dream. These four young people were actually going to Burma; the sailing date had been set. Everyone wanted to help.

The Hasseltine and Atwood homes in Bradford and Haverhill were busy with hasty wedding preparations. Deacon Hasseltine was still a little confused; even now he could hardly believe that his favorite Ann would soon be leaving him. Mrs. Hasseltine found little time for her reading: be it Burma or Boston, no daughter of hers was leaving home without a proper, sensible New England trousseau! In this she included a dozen pairs each of half-boots and laced ankle boots, for like all the Hasseltines, she believed in buying in bulk.

An order had been sent through to a store in Boston for the latest in white satin scoop bridal bonnets. Ann could hardly wait for the stagecoach to bring it. She was too excited even to be much help with the cooking, but hasty wedding though it would be, there would still be many extra mouths to feed.

There was only one disappointment; her future mother-in-law and father-in-law would not be coming. With the *Caravan* due to sail on February 10, there would hardly be time for Adoniram's elderly parents to make the trying winter journey to Bradford. Instead he had ridden horseback to Plymouth to make his farewells. Ann had heard so much about the Reverend Adoniram Judson, and of how his first-born son, her husband-to-be, had always been the apple of his eye. It was only natural that she was curious to meet her future in-laws, including his brother Elnathan and sister Abigail, but there was no time.

Although the Judsons were very much in favor of Adoniram's marriage to Ann, when they thought of his leaving for Burma they were torn with grief at parting with him for what might well be for ever. Yet he would be carrying that same Christian faith which in New England his father had been preaching for so long, to a people who had never heard of Jesus Christ. Although secretly the senior Judsons might wish that their son was not going, outwardly they were forced to admit that his intentions were of the finest, for they would further the gospel.

It was a sad little visit. Adoniram had, all his life, a horror of bidding anyone farewell, which sometimes caused him to be accused of thoughtlessness. Eventually he slipped away one snowy morning while his parents slept.

On February 5, 1812, in the same west room where they had met over a deep-dish chicken pie, Ann Hasseltine, wearing the precious white satin scoop bridal bonnet, married the young minister who had fallen in love with her on

43

sight. Parson Jonathan Allen, who had first introduced them, performed the simple ceremony, wearing his familiar old-fashioned black velvet suit, black silk stockings and shoes with large silver buckles. Pale winter sunshine filtered into the large pleasant room as Ann, showing little sign of nervousness, promised to love, honor and obey Adoniram. Deacon Hasseltine, endeavoring to appear happy, gave his daughter away. Most of the neighbors were present, for Ann had been popular in Bradford. It seemed impossible that she would soon be going out of their lives. There were as many eyes fastened upon the bridegroom as upon the bride. Both young people were rather enjoying the attention. Adoniram kept nervously brushing his unruly chestnut hair back from his forehead. He noticed with pride that Ann wore the silver watch that he had given her soon after their first meeting.

After the ceremony Ann's mother, helped by her other daughters, began to serve the wedding feast.

In the *Merrimack Intelligencer,* the newspaper of the time then read in the Haverhill district, there was no mention of the marriage in the next issue following the wedding day and published February 8. However, on the fifteenth of the same month there is a notice under *Marriages* of the wedding of Nancy Hasseltine "in Bradford." The date of the ceremony was not given.

Later on the wedding day Parson Allen preached, in Haverhill Church, a sermon which was especially directed at Ann and Harriet, both of whom he had known from childhood. Often he had watched them dancing with the other young people in the Hasseltines' frolic room.

He told Ann and Harriet that as missionaries' wives they would have a special duty to the women of India or Burma, whichever country their husbands might be serving in. To convert these women, he instructed them, "will be your business, my dear children, to whom your husbands can have little or no access. Go then, and do all in your power to enlighten their minds, and bring them to the knowledge of the truth. . . . Teach them to realize that they are not an inferior race of creatures, but stand upon a par with men. Teach them that they have immortal souls; and are no longer to burn themselves in the same fire with the bodies of their departed husbands."

Shuddering, the congregation turned their eyes on the two young women. Ann was still wearing her wedding bonnet. That evening many a Haverhill and Bradford matron was grateful for the safety of her own quiet fireside.

four

Ann felt like a thief in the night as she turned for one last look at the bedroom that had been hers so long. The pearwood chest at the foot of the curly maple bed; the stiff, formal painting of her brother John who had perished at sea; the honey-colored tallboy opposite the window.

Her parents' door was closed; that of her sister Mary a little ajar. How she longed to say good-by, but Adoniram was already halfway down the stairs. He hated good-bys. She had reasoned with him, but it was no good. "Partings are always painful," he told her. "This way is best for all."

Outside the air was crisp and dry. Heavy snow had fallen during the night. She shivered and looked back once more at the warm security of home. Adoniram helped her up into the carriage. He tugged at the reins and they were away.

It was slow going; the snow was deep. The horses were unsure of themselves. They had hardly reached the covered bridge leading over the Merrimack when a single rider caught up with them from behind.

"Father!" Ann sensed the color rise in her cheeks in spite of the intense cold.

Deacon Hasseltine had flung a long cloak over his nightshirt. When he liked he could be just as determined as Adoniram.

"You'll come home and say good-by properly," he informed the runaways. Adoniram opened his mouth, but for the second time in his life because of a Hasseltine no words came. Instead he returned meekly with Ann and her father.

There was no time for annoyance, though Adoniram found himself the object of a few black looks from Mrs. Hasseltine and Mary. "Why, not only were you going without bidding us farewell; you were leaving behind half your trousseau." Mrs. Hasseltine pointed to the hatboxes covered with gaily colored hand-blocked wallpaper, and the pine chest bearing the newly carved initials A.H.J. that stood waiting in the parlor.

Adoniram apologized and Mrs. Hasseltine shook hands with him. Then he was handed a large tin box. "You don't deserve it," she said, "but I know you like my gingerbread. Keep the lid on tight and it will stay fresh for months."

The bridegroom grinned. "He looks too boyish for a missionary," decided his new mother-in-law. "Well, at least he has high spirits like Ann." She thought of the quiet reserve of Samuel and Harriet. The two couples were as different as chalk from cheese.

48

At last the good-bys were over. When the Judsons were gone Deacon Hasseltine went into the barn on the pretense that he wanted to see how one of the cows who was due to calve was faring. Rebecca Hasseltine sank into the wing chair by the kitchen fire. Mary stirred the embers into a blaze, then hung over the flames the copper teakettle that John had given them. "I'll make you some tea, Mother," she said. "I've a notion that long after we are gone the world will remember our Ann."

Rebecca Hasseltine nodded. She was determined not to cry. "Ann could never be still, even as a little one," she recalled, her voice hardly more than a whisper. "I used to tell her that some day I hoped she would be satisfied with her rambling."

All roads led to Salem that sixth day of February, eighteen hundred and twelve; from Boston, Andover, Manchester, Gloucester, to name but a few places. On foot, horseback and by sleigh, men, women and children had made it a holiday, their mecca the great white Tabernacle Church where the first American missionaries to the Far East were that day to be ordained.

A group of young students from the Academy and Theological Seminary at Andover had walked sixteen miles through deep snow to attend. On the long walk back, one Academy boy collapsed from the cold and would have frozen to death by the wayside had not some theological students found him. In years to come this boy, William Goodell, was himself to serve as a missionary in Turkey.

During the ordination ceremonies each future missionary was blessed by an act known as "the laying on of hands."

Ann left her box pew and knelt quietly in the aisle to be close to her husband for this climax in the service.

It was a soul-stirring occasion. According to the *Salem Gazette* "appropriate music" was played on a "bass viol." Hundreds of well-wishers wanted to shake Ann's hand. Exhausted, she left with Adoniram to await the sailing of the *Caravan* at the home of her sister Rebecca, who had married the Reverend Joseph Emerson of Beverly.

Back at Haverhill in the best parlor of her mother's big white house, the fragile Harriet Atwood, who had listened with such awe to Ann's reading from Michael Symes' journal of the wonders of Burma, was married to quiet Samuel Newell.

Meantime, finances for the missionary endeavor were definitely improving. For miles around ministers, laymen and theological students went from door to door asking for gifts. A purse containing fifty dollars was thrown through the doorway of the Emerson home, labeled "For Mr. Judson's private use."

Before the *Caravan* actually sailed, over six thousand dollars were in the treasury, not to mention such practical gifts as clothing and food for the journey.

Of course not everybody was in favor of the missionary enterprise. One irate resident of Haverhill was moved to say in a letter to a friend residing in Portugal:

. . . these four foolish and inexperienced young people are about to embark, and will actually sail to the far-distant shores of Hindoostan, and marvellous to tell, to teach that numerous and ancient people the right way to heaven!

But things like this could never daunt the ardor of Adoniram Judson. Both Ann and he had met the *Caravan's* twenty-seven year old captain, Augustine Heard, in whom its owner, Mr. Dodge, had complete confidence.

The Judsons and Newells made it their business to pay several visits to the ship while it was waiting for a favorable time to sail. They inspected their cabins, watched the bigger luggage and many gifts being stowed away, and of course talked with the captain.

Ann was particularly amused by the large number of items he was asked "to pick up for friends" in the distant East. Red carnelian necklaces, cashmere shawls, straw mats, lengths of material, jars of preserved ginger and even two "palompons" suitable for the covering of a large double bed!

Captain Heard took these commissions "in stride" including the missionaries, although actually he was not much older than they.

"Why, it's Noah's Ark," was Ann Judson's remark when she first saw the *Caravan*'s deck, which was filled with a motley collection of pig pens and chicken coops, their inhabitants making a din reminiscent of a small farmyard.

Mr. Dodge, the ship's owner, made it his business to write out explicit instructions for his young captain on how to feed the livestock, including the missionaries.

"The yellow corn is for the fowls, the old white corn for the hogs." For the missionaries his orders were: ". . . give a fresh dish once a week or oftener, if practicable, and puddings, rice, etc."

The *Caravan* had lain all this time at the end of Crowninshield's Wharf. She was expected to be the last ship to embark from Salem for the Orient until after the expected war. Pickering Dodge made sure she was taking as much as her ninety-foot length and two hundred and sixty-seven tons would allow. However, the tenth of February came and went. On the thirteenth she slowly sailed out of the wharf for the center of the harbor.

Still the sailing was delayed. Wet, snowy and stormy, the weather was not being helpful at all. Adoniram and Ann had moved to the Kimball house where she had stayed before during her time at Salem. It was then February 18. They had hardly arrived when news was brought them that they would sail on the full tide that same afternoon.

Adoniram could hardly contain his natural high spirits or excitement. Not waiting for Ann to help him, he flung their just-unpacked pieces of small personal luggage into bags and boxes and took them to Crowninshield's Wharf in a sleigh. On returning to the Kimball house he was dismayed to find it filled with friends who had come to say farewell. To escape good-bys, he returned alone to the wharf, found himself a boat and was rowed out to the *Caravan*. There Ann found him.

It was a bitterly cold day with a biting wind. Well-meaning friends found it impossible to stand for long on the freezing wharf. The afternoon went by and still the *Caravan* could not sail. The Judsons, Newells and two young male students who decided to keep them company overnight went below to the cabins.

The experience was a new one for Ann. She listened to the harbor waves lapping at the side of the vessel, the creaking of the timbers, the cry of the wind through the naked masts.

Then she heard her companions joyfully singing:

> *"Landed safe in distant regions,*
> *Tell the Burmans Jesus died;*
> *Tell them Satan and his legions*
> *Bow to Him they crucified.*

"Far beyond the mighty Ganges,
When vast floods beyond us roll,
Think how widely Jesus ranges
Nations wide from pole to pole."

five

They were all seasick at first. When they felt well enough, Ann and Harriet noted the unpleasant fact in their journals. Poor Harriet was most sick of all; in fact she quite thought she was dying. As the wooden vessel rose and fell on the enormous Atlantic breakers even Ann, who was not as sick as her friend, felt bound to record that she "had many distressing apprehensions of death." Further she wrote that she "felt unwilling to die on the sea, not so much on account of my state after death, as the dreadfulness of perishing amid the waves." In all honesty Ann added that she had not been as sick as she expected to be; "no worse, through the whole, than if I had taken a gentle emetic."

Sickness was not their only trouble, for after five days at

sea the brig sprang a bad leak and although all hands were called to the pumps, passengers included, it nearly sank. Fortunately the hole was found at last and plugged. Another week passed and even the missionaries were enjoying the voyage. The sickness was gone and, after all, the two young couples were on their honeymoon.

The only lasting difficulty was the food. In spite of Pickering Dodge's explicit instructions regarding variation of meals, the food did not seem the same as at home. "Everything tasted differently from what it does on land and those things I was most fond of at home, I loathed the most here," Ann noted. At last they concluded that the heavy, full feeling in their stomachs was due to lack of exercise. Walking was the remedy, they decided, but a deck full of chicken coops and pigpens was hardly suitable. Skipping was the alternative. A rope was found and, like children in school, the missionaries skipped for hours at a time. Finally, tiring of so monotonous a form of exercise, they decided to dance instead. It was much more fun, reminding the girls of their old carefree days in the Hasseltine frolics room at Bradford. The weather turned warmer and with it came better appetites, although Harriet was still a little off-color. She could not face coffee or tea without milk, and was always craving types of food that were not available aboard a sailing ship. By now she was sure she was going to have a baby, deciding it would be born in India or Burma that November. She was more excited than frightened at the prospect of having her first child in a foreign land.

The crew of the *Caravan* never failed to amaze Ann, who during her stay in Salem must frequently have overheard strong sailorly language. She wrote in her journal, "I have not heard the least profane language since I have been on board the vessel. This is very uncommon."

She was now enjoying the voyage very much. Even the first wave of homesickness had passed, although there were moments when Captain Heard pointed out on his compass the direction of Bradford that she felt a little twinge at her heart. As for Adoniram, she found him to be "the kindest" of husbands.

On Sundays, with the permission of Captain Heard, who usually attended with two of his officers, services were held in the double cabin. Sometimes a ship would be sighted and the *Caravan* pass so close that people could easily be seen on the distant deck. Captain Heard did not communicate with any strange vessels because of the possibility of war between the United States and Britain. As warmer temperatures were encountered Ann and Harriet were introduced to the pleasures of bathing daily in salt water.

When May came the *Caravan* had already crossed the Equator. They were sailing round the Cape of Good Hope; the weather had turned wet and cold. At this time Harriet wrote in a letter which after their finally landing in India was sent to her mother:

I care not how soon we reach Calcutta, and are placed in a still room, with a bowl of milk and a loaf of Indian bread. I can hardly think of this simple fare without exclaiming, oh, what a luxury. I have been so weary of the excessive rocking of the vessel, and the almost intolerable smell after the rain, that I have done little more than lounge on the bed for several days. But I have been blest with excellent spirits, and to-day have been running about the deck, and *dancing* in our room for *exercise,* as well as ever.

While studying at the seminary in Andover, Adoniram had been working on a New Testament translation from the original Greek. He had brought it along to continue

57

during the voyage. There was one particular word that troubled his conscience. This was the Greek word most often translated as "baptism."

Born a Congregationalist, he had been baptized as a tiny baby in the usual manner by having a few drops of water sprinkled on his head, yet nowhere in the whole of the New Testament could he find a description of anybody being baptized by sprinkling. John the Baptist used total immersion in the River Jordan for believers; even Christ was baptized by this method. The more Adoniram looked at the Greek word for baptism, the more unhappy he became over its true meaning.

As was only natural he confided his searchings to Ann, conceding ruefully that it certainly looked as if their own Congregationalists were wrong and the Baptists right.

Ann was very troubled. By this time she had learned that it was futile to argue with her young husband, yet the uncomfortable fact remained: the American Congregationalists were sending them as missionaries to the Far East and paying their salaries. What would happen if Adoniram "changed horses in midstream"? Baptists and Congregationalists in New England were on friendly terms. How embarrassing it would be if the newly appointed Congregationalist missionaries should suddenly switch their own beliefs in order to embrace Baptist teachings!

"If you become a Baptist, I will not," Ann informed her husband, but sweeping her threat aside Adoniram continued to search for an answer to the personal dilemma in which he found himself.

By early June they were a hundred miles off the coast of Ceylon, by which time all four missionaries were hardened seafarers. Even Harriet could boldly write, "I know not how it is; but I hear the thunder roll; see the lightning flash; and the waves threatening to swallow up the vessel; and yet remain unmoved."

Ann thrilled to the sight of a delicate butterfly and two strange tropical birds. Land was near, and on June 12, one hundred and fourteen days after leaving America, they actually saw, twenty miles away, the coast of Orissa.

Captain Heard gave orders for the ship to be anchored in the Bay of Bengal until he could obtain the services of a reputable pilot to steer her through the shallow waters.

Sometimes ships waited for days for such a man, but Captain Heard was lucky. Next day a ship arrived with an English pilot, his leadsman, an English youth, and the first Hindu the Judsons and Newells had ever seen. A little man with "a dark copper color" skin, he was wearing "calico trousers and a white cotton short gown." Ann was plainly disappointed in his appearance. "He looks as feminine as you can imagine," she decided.

The pilot possessed excellent skill at his calling; all day long the *Caravan* slowly made her way through the difficult passages. Alas, to Ann's consternation, his language while thus employed left much to be desired. He swore so loudly at the top of his voice, that she didn't get any sleep all the next night.

Next morning the *Caravan* was out of the treacherous Bay. Relieved of the major part of his responsibility for the safety of the ship, the pilot's oaths became fewer. Slowly she moved up the Hooghli River, a mouth of the mighty Ganges, toward Calcutta.

Ann was entranced with the view, as were her husband and friends. Running across the deck, which was empty now that the livestock had been killed and eaten, they sniffed the spice-laden breezes that came from the shore, each pointing out new and exciting wonders to the other.

Out came the journal and in it went Ann's own description of the scene:

"On each side of the Hoogli, where we are now sailing, are the Hindoo cottages, as thick together as the houses in our seaports. They are very small, and in the form of haystacks, without either chimney or windows. They are situated in the midst of trees, which hang over them, and appear truly romantick. The grass and fields of rice are perfectly green, and herds of cattle are everywhere feeding on the banks of the river, and the natives are scattered about, differently employed. Some are fishing, some driving the team, and many are sitting indolently on the banks of the river. The pagodas we have passed are much larger than the houses."

Harriet was just as delighted. Where were the hardships she had expected? She was certain now that it would be no harder to bear her child here in such pleasant surroundings than at home in the big white house in Haverhill. With childlike innocence she wrote of the Indians as "walking with fruit and umbrellas in their hands, with the tawny children around them. . . . This is the most delightful *trial* I have ever had," she decided.

The Indians who came aboard ship to collect the mail also interested her greatly, even if she was suitably shocked, according to the customs of the society in which she had been reared, to find them "naked, except a piece of cotton cloth wrapped around their middle."

At last they saw Calcutta, largest city of Bengal and the *Caravan's* destination. Founded August 24, 1690 by Job Charnock of the East India Company, and commonly called "The City of Palaces," it seemed a vast and elegant place to Ann Hasseltine Judson. Solid brick buildings painted dazzling white, large domes and tall, picturesque palms stretched as far as the eye could see, while the wharves and harbor were filled with tall-masted sailing ships. The noise stunned her. Crowds flocked through the waterfront streets chattering loudly in their strange-sounding Bengali tongue.

Harriet's mouth watered with anticipation when after months of dreaming she sat down at last to her much-craved milk and fresh bread. Ann, pleased to see her friend happy, was intrigued by the new fruits a friend of Captain Heard had sent on board for their enjoyment. Cautiously she sampled her first pineapple and another fruit whose taste she likened to that of "a rich pear." Though she did not then know its name, this strange new fruit was a banana.

six

The first act of Adoniram and Samuel on reaching Calcutta was to report at the police station, a necessity when landing in East India Company territory. On the way they tried to discover all they could about Burma, and they were disturbed to find that Michael Symes's book had not presented an altogether true picture. He had failed to realize that the Burmese were not really treating him as the important visitor he considered himself. They were in fact quietly laughing at him, for their King wished to have nothing to do with the Western world. When Captain John Gibault of Salem had visited Burma in 1793 his ship, the *Astra,* had been promptly commandeered and taken by her captors up the Irrawaddy River. Although after much trouble he did manage to get it back, he discovered there was no trade to be had. All Captain Gibault took back to Salem were a few items for the town's East India Museum. A year later another Salem ship returned from Burma with a cargo of gum lacquer which nobody wanted to buy. After that Salem ships decided to bypass unfriendly Burma.

The Burmese appeared to have little knowledge of British power or any idea of trade. They despised foreigners. Cruel Burmese governors could, on the slightest whim, take a man's life. As for missionaries, even if they succeeded in getting into the country they probably would not be allowed to preach the Christian faith to the Burmans. Unspeakable tortures or even execution might well be their fate.

"Go back to America or any other place," well-meaning friends of Captain Heard advised them, "but put thoughts of going to Burma out of your heads."

Somewhat daunted, the two American missionaries reached the police station where they were questioned by a most unfriendly clerk. When he discovered they had received from the Company's Court of Directors no permission to live in India, coupled with the fact that they were Americans who had been sent to Asia to convert "the heathen," he became more belligerent than ever.

They explained that they desired only to stop in India until a ship traveling on to Burma could be found. However, because of the difficulties in that country of which they had only just learned, their stay might be a little longer than they had at first expected.

The clerk did eventually give them certificates to show that they had complied with regulations by registering at

64

the police station, stressing that it was extremely unlikely they would be allowed to remain long in India.

Before returning to their wives, who were still blissfully eating bananas and unaware of any difficulties, the two young men paid a call on Dean William Carey of the pioneer group of English Baptist missionaries whose headquarters were at Serampore.

Carey was in Calcutta by permission of the East India Company, although they disapproved of his mission. He had been appointed a professor of Oriental Languages in the Fort William college, a job which he gladly took in order to obtain from the Company a more tolerant recognition of the work being done by the Serampore Baptists. The son of a poor English cobbler, Carey worked first in India as superintendent of an indigo plantation before realizing his great ambition to become a missionary. He had personally translated the Gospel into Bengali, a fact which had won him Adoniram's immediate admiration and respect.

Dean Carey also was emphatic that the Judsons and Newells should put Burma right out of their minds. His son Felix was already living there and, although married to a woman of Burmese origin, found life well nigh impossible. The viceroy in Rangoon allowed him to stay only because he thought he had come to minister to the spiritual needs of the few Europeans also living in the seaport. He had not the faintest idea that Felix wanted to convert the Burmese.

So much for Burma. As for India, even for British subjects the missionary calling was made difficult—and they were Americans. The East India Company did not want missionaries preaching a gospel that could be interpreted as subversive and revolutionary. They wished to keep the natives in ignorance of western ideas which might well lead to disturbances and revolt. Besides, the Company found the sale to Indians of small idols made in England a profitable source of income. It was not until a year after the unpleasant experiences of the Judsons and Newells in India that, owing to the efforts of a number of Christian men, the charter of the East India Company was amended by Act of Parliament in London to insure better treatment of missionaries.

Next day Adoniram and Newell returned once more to the police station, this time with the kindly Captain Heard, who found himself the recipient of a stern dressing-down for bringing American missionaries to India without any formal permission of the government. The Calcutta newspapers had published the names of the *Caravan's* passenger list with their occupations: *Missionaries*. It seemed that the police clerk of the day before had not reported to his superior the fact of the American's visit.

The night that followed was their last aboard the *Caravan*. The missionaries had two offers of accommodation. One was made by Captain Heard, who had rented a house in the city from which he would do his own business, but they felt they had already caused him enough trouble. Instead, the hospitality of Dr. Carey's home was accepted. That afternoon they left the *Caravan*.

Although both girls had fretted to go ashore, when eventually they did, everything seemed strange and frightening. Ann found herself alone in a *palanquin,* a covered couch supported on poles resting on the bearers' shoulders. Never before had she heard such a babel of tongues and seen so many carriages or streets so crowded with people. It was a nightmare, and to complicate matters Adoniram had strutted off to Dr. Carey's house on his own. The native bearers ran so fast that Ann lost sight of him almost immediately. All sorts of terrible thoughts rushed through her mind. Would she ever see him again? Wasn't this the scene of the Black Hole of Calcutta where one hundred and forty-six English prisoners were confined one burning summer's night, and all but twenty-three of them perished? She now understood why "no English lady is here seen walking the streets"; it wouldn't be safe, she decided. Then with a slight bump the *palanquin* was lowered to the ground and she was looking at a large white house that impressed her as being more like a palace than a private residence.

Eventually Adoniram arrived, making Ann forget her moments of near-panic in the *palanquin*. Together with Harriet she explored the enormous building, any room of which was larger than their entire home back in New England. There were no fireplaces, and there was no glass in the windows. Servants were everywhere, so many that they were always getting in the way. Each servant had his own appointed task and would do no other. Ann noted that one might sweep a room but would never think of dusting it. This was reserved for another.

That evening Ann attended a religious service according to the rites of the Church of England, where she heard with delight the organ play "Bangor," her favorite tune. The sermon was good but Ann was far more taken with the enormous *punkah* fans hanging from the church ceiling, which were operated by Indian boys pulling on ropes. She mentioned them in her journal as "punkies."

Next day she had her first introduction to child marriage, watching a ten-year-old bridegroom riding in his own *palanquin* to be married. The same afternoon she left by boat together with her husband and the Newells for Serampore which was fifteen miles distant. Before leaving they all signed a letter of thanks to Captain Heard, which bore the postscript, "We wish that we could make some suitable return for your goodness, but as this is far out of our power, we can only express our feelings."

The Serampore Mission possessed a garden that immediately took Ann's nature-conscious eye. She had never before seen so many varieties of plant life cultivated in one spot, and reported that it was "as far superior to any in America, as the best garden in America is to a common farmer's."

Although Deacon Hasseltine's daughter had herself been reared on a farm, she could not be blamed for her ignorance of the fact that Dr. Carey was a keen horticulturist who for over ten years had acquired for his mission garden specimens from all over the world.

She was fascinated, although somewhat shocked, by a ceremony honoring Jagannath or Juggernaut, the Hindu god, whose name means "Lord of the World," to which she journeyed by *budgerow*—a boat containing a cushioned room hung with Venetian-type blinds.

The enormous wooden image with black face, red body and arms of gilt had eyes formed of brilliant stones. It was hung with garlands and the extended red mouth reached almost from ear to ear. Brought out of his temple, Jagannath was taken to the sacred waters of the Ganges and bathed. Although she noted that the pilgrims "poured muddy water down their children's throats" Ann seems to have been spared the spectacle, then prevalent, of pilgrims throwing themselves under the wheels of the cart on which Jagannath was mounted, in the firm belief that this form of death would help bring them to heaven.

On July 1 word reached the Americans that filled each

of them with consternation. The men were told to report at once to the police station, where they were ordered to return at once to America on the *Caravan*.

At once they petitioned Lord Minto, the Governor General, but with no effect. Finally on July 15 they were forbidden by the police to attempt missionary activities in any British dominion or territory belonging to an ally of Britain, which included Java and all the East Indian Islands. If they could find a ship willing to take them farther afield they need not return to America.

If officialdom was uncharitable to the young people, individual Britons were not, for while the two missionaries were still in the police station an East India Company chaplain arrived with five hundred rupees which he handed to Samuel Newell as a gift from Calcutta friends sympathetic to missions.

They did not know where to go. Burma seemed more impossible than ever. Recently Felix Carey himself had been forced to flee to an English man-of-war lying off Rangoon because a general massacre was threatened. Five hundred men had been buried alive by their commander for having the audacity to be recruits sent him by an officer he did not like.

Terrible punishments such as beheading, crucifixion or pouring melted lead down the throat were inflicted, they were told, for the most trivial offences.

Adoniram considered going to China, but there the prospects were as bleak as in Burma. For teaching Christianity in that vast country the penalty was death.

Then came a faint ray of hope. The governor of the Isle of France, now known as Mauritius, which lay five thousand miles to the southwest, would welcome missionaries. Furthermore, a ship, the *Colonel Gillespie,* was due to sail in four days but the captain could only be persuaded to take two passengers.

The Judsons at once decided that their companions should be the ones to go. Harriet's baby was due in less than three months. If it were to be born on land she must travel at once.

The *Colonel Gillespie* was a little overdue in sailing but Harriet filled every minute to its full capacity. She went shopping, attended numerous teas and suppers given by well-meaning sympathizers, and finally arrived aboard ship completely worn out.

In spite of all their difficulties with the East India Company, Adoniram was still troubled over the Baptist question. Every so often the old worries and doubts would well up in his mind, demanding to be answered. Were the Congregationalists wrong and the Baptists right over the actual methods of baptism? Ann was torn between loyalty to her husband and that of the denomination in which she had been raised and in which of course her own father was a deacon. She wrote at the time, "I tried to have him give it up, and rest satisfied in his old sentiments. He, however, said he felt it his duty to examine closely a subject on which he felt so many doubts."

In her own personal quandary Ann also began to search the Bible for a few words in favor of infant baptism. Unhappily she could find none. Reluctantly she finally admitted to Adoniram that he might be right, at the same time noting that

Mr. J. feels convinced from Scripture, that he has never been baptized, and that he cannot conscientiously administer baptism to infants. This change of sentiment must necessarily produce a separation. As we are perfectly united with our brethren in every other respect, and are much attached to them, it is inexpressibly painful to leave them, and go alone to a separate station.

The decision was made. On September 6, 1812, in the Lal Bazar Chapel, Calcutta, Adoniram and Ann Judson were baptized by total immersion, the Reverend William Ward performing the ceremony. Ann recorded,

Thus we are confirmed Baptists, not because we wanted to be, but because truth compelled us to be. We have endeavored to count the cost, and be prepared for the many severe trials resulting from this change of sentiment. We anticipate the loss of reputation, and of the affection and esteem of many of our American friends. But the most trying circumstance attending this change, and that which has caused us most pain, is the separation which must take place between us and our dear missionary associates . . . We feel that we are alone in the world, with no real friend but each other, no-one on whom we can depend but God.

With the Baptist question settled, the Judsons were more eager than ever to find a boat so that they could join the Newells as soon as possible.

seven

"*Cutcha pho, anna sahib; cutcha pho, anna.* Never fear, madam; never fear."

The native sailors of the pilot boat on which she was traveling down river tried to reassure her but Ann could not help feeling alarmed. She watched the crew hoist a large top-heavy sail. As it billowed out in the wind she was sure the boat would capsize, spilling them all out into the choppy water.

How she longed for an umbrella; the sun overhead was scorching hot. The pilot boat was hurrying after *La Belle Créole* upon which the Judsons were hoping to sail and eventually join the Newells in the Isle of France. They had been forced to leave Calcutta under cover of darkness, for the authorities had suddenly decided to send them to England. They were even suspected of being American spies posing as missionaries.

Unable to obtain the necessary pass to sail on *La Belle Créole,* they had to get aboard unseen. The gates of the dockyards were usually securely locked at night but on this particular occasion they had been left open. A bribe in the necessary quarters had worked the trick so that the Judsons, with a number of hired coolies to carry their luggage, passed safely through.

After that all seemed to go according to plan. The ship sailed slowly down the Hooghli River and after three days they began to feel sure they had escaped safely. Then they were hailed from their cabin in the middle of the night to be met with the awful news that a dispatch had arrived from Calcutta ordering *La Belle Créole* to drop anchor and lay ready to be searched "as passengers were on board who had been ordered to England."

Adoniram promptly took refuge in an English tavern ashore, leaving Ann aboard with the baggage. Worried and nervous, she decided to join him later that night when she found that he had heard of another friendly tavern at Fultah, sixteen miles further downstream. Perhaps they would be safe there until they could find another ship. Ann must return alone to *La Belle Créole* and get the luggage, for it was too dangerous for her husband to be seen.

The captain had a better suggestion. Ann could remain aboard with the luggage as far as Fultah. Even if the ship were searched he didn't think the authorities would worry about a woman. It was her husband they were really after.

Ann returned in the pilot boat to where Adoniram was anxiously waiting in the tavern with news of the arrangement; yet even while they were still talking *La Belle*

74

Créole's captain felt obliged to take advantage of a favorable wind. Quickly hoisting sail, his ship was already disappearing round a bend in the river. Springing into the pilot boat Ann left a worried husband ashore while she chased after their luggage.

After a nightmare journey they caught up with *La Belle Créole,* and the luggage was recovered. Ann was later landed at Fultah with only a few rupees in her pocket. Trying to appear more at ease than she felt, Ann entered the tavern, which was kept by an Englishman, and asked for a room. There, close to tears, she sat wondering if she would ever see Adoniram again. A terrible wave of homesickness came over her. Here she was, hunted like a criminal, knowing only a few words of the language, alone at a waterside tavern in India.

Her fears for Adoniram's safety were put to rest when he arrived at nightfall in a small skiff. Then providence itself seemed to take a hand, for while they were at supper a letter was brought them by the tavern owner. Inside was a magistrate's pass to rejoin the ship. They never knew the name of the person who had procured it on their behalf.

But *La Belle Créole* might already have passed out of the bounds of the river and be headed for the open sea. There was just one chance that like other vessels she could have anchored seventy miles downstream at the port of Saugur for a final overhaul before sailing out into the open Bay of Bengal.

Then followed another hectic boat ride to rejoin the ship, only this time Ann was not alone; her beloved Adoniram was with her. Of it she wrote

It was a most dreary night for me but Mr. J. slept the greater part of the night. The next day we had a favor-

75

able wind, and before night reached Saugur where were many ships at anchor, and among the rest we had the happiness to find the *Créole*. She had been anchored there two days, waiting for some of the ship's crew. I never enjoyed a sweeter moment in my life, than when I was sure we were in sight of the *Créole*.

Seven weeks later they sighted the Isle of France and Ann, clinging happily to her husband's arm, impatiently waited to be taken ashore where she was sure Harriet and the new baby, now at least two months old, would be waiting to greet them. Besides, she had some exciting news of her own to tell Harriet. Another baby was on the way. She pressed Adoniram's arm lovingly as a small boat came alongside to collect them.

A moment or two later came the terrible, unbelievable news: Both Harriet and the baby were dead.

It was some little time before they heard the whole tragic story and even then Samuel Newell was too broken up to give them all the details at once. Harriet, exhausted by her last-minute excursions in Calcutta, had been taken with a fever almost before their ship had sailed. Recovering after a week she was later attacked "with severe pains in the stomach and bowels, the disease of the country" (probably dysentery). Again she rallied, and then on October 8, only two days before her nineteeth birthday, Harriet Atwood Newell became the mother of a little girl. Of the birth she managed feebly to write that it took place "on the cabin floor with no other attendant but my dear Mr. Newell."

Five days later the ship was caught in a terrible storm. Rain poured into the cabins, drenching the passengers to the skin, including the baby. The infant took cold from the sudden exposure, dying in Harriet's arms. Even this was not the worst. From that moment Harriet's always fragile health rapidly deteriorated. Daily she seemed to waste away in a manner in which she was quick to recognize the symptoms of tuberculosis, the disease that had carried off her father and other close relatives. She insisted to her husband that she would die and that he must help her prepare by prayer for her new life in a better world. Newell was grief-stricken, refusing to believe that her short life was ending. In the lonely weeks that followed he remembered with gratitude that not once did Harriet say she was frightened; neither was she unduly sad except at leaving him behind, but to one of such strong Christian convictions this, she maintained, was only for a little while. Besides, she was sure that in heaven there would be a happy reunion with her lost child.

When at the beginning of November the *Gillespie* landed at Port Louis, Newell had her taken at once to a little house that he had rented. Two doctors attended her but their efforts were in vain. Eventually even Newell gave up hope. On November 30 Harriet died, the first casualty of the gallant little enterprise that had left Salem with so many hopeful expectations. She was buried next day under the shade of an evergreen tree in the Port Louis Cemetery.

Although Ann was prostrate with grief, she tried to comfort Samuel Newell, who was a broken man. Time and again her thoughts strayed to that afternoon—now it seemed an eternity ago—when she had found in Harriet such an interested listener to her reading from Michael Symes's Burmese narrative. At times she wondered if she were even indirectly to blame for her best friend's early death, for if she had not filled Harriet's mind with such glowing thoughts of adventure in a strange, exotic land perhaps even now she would be safely home in friendly Haverhill . . . But then she thought of the happy days on the *Caravan*, of how much in love Harriet and Samuel had been. Brief though their marriage was, it had been filled with mutual love and understanding. They must think of Harriet as a martyr, she told the bereaved Samuel. She would have been the last to wish them to weep and mourn. Just the same, when Ann was alone with her own thoughts she took up her pen and sadly wrote, "I am left behind, still to endure the trials of a missionary life. O that this severe dispensation may be sanctified to my soul and that I may be prepared to follow my dear departed sister."

After a few days of mourning, Ann and her husband forced themselves to be practical and to think about starting their own mission. The island's governor was a friendly man and in rather an amused voice confessed he had been told to "have an eye on those American missionaries." Where were they to start work? That was the pressing question. It was not long before Adoniram had to confess that there was no place in which to preach on the Isle of France except the local army barracks or hospital. He found that the island's population was principally composed of slaves to whom their owners refused religious instruction. The Isle of France was not suitable for the kind of mission Ann and he had planned.

The cruelty of the slaveowners was horrifying. One evening Ann was disturbed by a great commotion in the yard of her temporary home, which connected with the property of another family. Running to the door, she saw a female slave, her hands tied, being beaten with a club by her irate mistress.

Ann, the blood running cold within her and altogether forgetting she was expecting a child, ran up to the owner de-

78

manding in broken French to know what the slave girl had done, and begging her to stop the beating.

The mistress told her that the slave had tried to escape, whereon Ann tactfully talked her into discontinuing the punishment, but not before the woman had thrown the club at the slave's head. All that night the slave girl lay out in the yard, her hands tied behind her. With much relief Ann saw them release her in the morning, when she was allowed to go about her usual duties.

When dusk fell Ann watched with mounting horror as into the yard was carried a large chain with a ring at one end large enough to go round the unfortunate slave's neck. Fixed to this ring, which was fastened by a lock and key, were two pieces of iron about an inch wide and four inches long, which were arranged to prevent the poor creature from eating.

Then the mistress appeared and once more started to beat the slave. Again Ann interfered. By this time the half-crazed owner was white with anger. Ann managed at last to calm her, and asked if she could not forgive her servant.

Whether it was the American girl's extreme youth or frankness of approach that impressed the French slaveowner it is hard to say, but impress her she did. The beating stopped and the chain with its awful collar was taken away. Flushed, the mistress told her slave that she was being forgiven only because Mme. Judson had requested it. The slave took one look at Ann and fell on her knees, crying, "Merci, madame!" and kissed her deliverer's feet.

Samuel Newell decided to sail for Ceylon. Adoniram was already planning to leave the island but again the question was, where should they go? Finally it was decided to try Penang, which would mean first going to Madras and risking the East India Company's wrath.

Just before they sailed on the *Countess of Harcourt* Ann made a pilgrimage to the remote cemetery where her friend Harriet was buried. Standing alone among the white, painted monuments and dark tropical greenery she was suddenly overcome with emotion. Almost bitterly she recorded her thoughts: "The visit revived many painful, solemn feelings. But a little while ago, she was with us on board ship, and joined us daily in prayer and praise. Now her body is crumbling to dust, in a land of strangers."

But she must not let her thoughts linger in the past, she decided as she left the remote cemetery, for she firmly believed that her own dear Harriet was safely in heaven.

On May 7, 1813 Ann embarked with Adoniram for Madras, arriving June 4. Here they were graciously welcomed by two English missionaries, a Mr. and Mrs. Loveless, but even there the East India Company continued to cast its ogrelike shadow across their lives. The police had already informed the supreme governor in Bengal of the American missionaries' return to India. Deportation would surely follow.

Desperate, Adoniram haunted the docks in search of a ship so that they might continue on to Penang while Ann, already in an advanced state of pregnancy, fretted her hours away at the Loveless's home.

Then once again providence stepped in. A ship bound for Burma was found!

eight

"Stay away from Burma." In vain the English missionaries together with other new acquaintances in Madras tried to advise the Judsons. "Think of the coming baby," they pleaded.

But Adoniram could not be convinced. If they were deported to England more time would be wasted. Already since they had left America months had passed without the remotest hope of starting a mission.

The *Georgiana*, "a crazy old vessel," was sailing under the Portuguese flag. Decrepit, smelly and dirty, it did not even have a proper cabin to offer its two passengers, so a sort of canvas shelter was erected for them upon the open deck. It seemed more than likely that Ann's baby would be born during the voyage, and remembering the fate of Harriet Newell under similar circumstances, Adoniram engaged a European woman to serve as a nurse. A big strapping person, seemingly in the best of health, she went aboard the vessel several days ahead of sailing to make the canvas "cabin" as comfortable as possible for the mother-to-be.

The Judsons themselves had barely boarded when the nurse fell in a fit to the deck, where she drew a few gasping breaths and died almost immediately. Apart from the shock of her unexpected death, there was no time to get a replacement. A few days out in rough water, Ann began to feel very sick indeed. There, with no more shelter from the broiling sun than a thin canvas roof, and only Adoniram in attendance, she gave birth to her first child. It was stillborn.

The baby was buried at sea while Ann, without medicines to help her, lingered on the brink of death. Adoniram never left her side but sat in a rough improvised seat beside her, from time to time wiping her brow and speaking words of comfort. Through the misty sea of pain it was always his reassuring smile that she saw. Afterwards she often said that it was to him she owed her life. The ship tossed and turned on the choppy, heaving waves; she could not even be kept on course. Instead of going to the Nicobar Islands to collect a cargo of coconuts she was driven into a dangerous strait between the Little and Great Andamans where even her captain had never previously ventured for fear of contact with the cannibals who were said to inhabit the savage coasts.

There was nothing to do but watch and pray. The water was filled with great black rocks so close to the surface that those on deck could see them clearly. Then something happened that doubtless saved the ship, and Ann in particular, for whom the continuously heaving waves were becoming a living death . . . All at once the sea became calm. The missionaries were not the only ones aboard who thought it a miracle.

The Portuguese captain was able to guide his creaking craft without mishap through the treacherous reefs. Once safely in the Andaman Sea they met with favorable Southern winds which gently guided them toward Rangoon. The captain was so relieved that he completely forgot the coconuts.

Ann, though terribly weak, was better. The sense of emptiness seemed the hardest thing to bear, her arms aching for the child they had never held. Adoniram consoled her as best he could. They were both young, he told her. There would be another baby, probably several. She tried to smile but the emptiness would not leave her.

Once more Adoniram looked hopefully forward to the country that for so long had filled his missionary dreams. Even the terrible tales he had been told of life in that vast exotic land were momentarily forgotten. Besides, his active mind was already filled with a new project. The Bible had never been translated into Burmese and he, Adoniram Judson, had appointed himself to do it.

While Ann still rested beneath the tentlike shelter, heartsick over the loss of her baby, Adoniram impatiently paced the ship's deck watching for the first glimpse of their promised land. On Thursday July 13, 1813, the creaking *Georgiana*, after being at sea three weeks, finally found the entrance to the Rangoon River, a mouth of the great Irrawaddy. Slowly she sailed past the waiting Burmese watchboat, engaged a pilot to guide her and then continued slowly on her way.

Adoniram's first sight of Burma was very disappointing.

Spread out on either side of the river bank was nothing but steaming swampland, reeking of dank straggly weeds and sickly, rotting date palms.

Where were the colorful inhabitants described in Michael Symes's book that had so thoroughly sown the seed of Burma in his fertile brain? Nowhere could he see a single glittering temple or painted ship of gold. Instead, the poverty-stricken fishing villages whose flimsy bamboo shacks clung like tentacles to the very marsh appeared only as a symbol of slow, lingering death and destruction. Sometimes he caught sight of a few half-naked inhabitants mending their nets. At last, sadly disillusioned, he went back to Ann. He had hardly sat down by her improvised bed when the cry went up: "Rangoon!"

Running toward the prow, he feasted his eyes for the first time on the golden spire of the Shwe-Dagon Pagoda, most famed of all Burma's many temples. His heart leapt for joy. This was something Ann must share. Hurrying back, he lifted her wasted body into his arms, carrying her onto the open deck to see for herself.

There was little or no comparison between the orderliness of the white stone buildings that lined the wharfs of Calcutta and the motley collection of teak and bamboo buildings in Rangoon. At first glance it seemed little more than a small, dirty town. Creeks filled with sluggish yellow water and slops threaded themselves between the huddle of shaky dwellings and rough, tumbledown warehouses.

There were three main wharves, a number of improvised landing cranes for cargo and a port-holed fort boasting about a dozen antiquated cannon.

The dinginess and smell of Rangoon cast a spell of depression over Adoniram, completely obliterating his recent excitement over the glory of the Shwe-Dagon Pagoda. Tired and sick at heart, he went ashore with the idea of finding the Felix Carey mission house, which he judged correctly to be a largish building standing just outside the city walls. However, at the last moment his courage failed him and, feeling very sorry for himself, he returned to his sick wife aboard the *Georgiana*. Ann later recalled, "It was the unhappiest day of our lives."

But sleep and the persistence of youth worked wonders with both of them. When it came time to go ashore next morning an armchair was found for Ann, who was still too weak to walk. Four Burmese men wearing nothing but loincloths knotted up in front slipped the bamboo poles through the chair and gently lifted it on their strong shoulders. This time Adoniram did not leave his wife alone, as he had done on their arrival in Calcutta, for which she was thankful. Instead he trotted along beside her.

The streets of Rangoon were narrow and dirty. A few were roughly paved with brick, while the homes themselves were mostly constructed of the ever-convenient bamboo. Even in India they had never seen so many temples or heard the tinkling sound of so many tiny pagoda bells. Saffron-robed priests with shaven heads, naked children smoking cigars and sad-faced lepers begging for alms formed part of the jostling, happy, arguing crowds through which they passed. The din was terrific; at times Ann felt it would split her throbbing head wide open.

Just inside the city walls the Burmese chair bearers decided to take a rest and enjoy a well-earned cigar. This was all the expectant crowd needed, especially the gaily dressed ladies. Englishmen they had seen occasionally, but an Englishwoman (they decided that Ann was English) was too unusual a curiosity to miss. Crowding around her armchair, they carefully examined her white skin, New England footwear and large scoop bonnet.

Sick as she was, Ann managed to muster a smile as they peered in, and even reached in to finger her black curls. The women, delighted with this response, went into loud peals of laughter. They then proceeded to discuss the strange white woman, wondered if she smoked cigars and conjectured about her personal habits. They decided she was interesting enough to be liked, while she had already come to the conclusion that their childlike frankness was equally pleasing. Ann smiled again, admiring the crimson silk petticoats of the women, together with the gorgeous flowers plaited into their carefully oiled hair. Then, refreshed by their rest, the bearers lifted the chair and hurried off to the custom house, which turned out to be a large open shed. Here, sitting on mats, the custom officers were already anticipating the Judsons' arrival.

The law required that a tenth of every cargo be set aside for the King, and so the baggage of any traveler was thoroughly inspected, handled, criticized, laughed over and sometimes, through such an overhauling, badly damaged.

Adoniram was stripped to the skin and his clothing thoroughly searched. Much to the delight of the women who had followed her, Ann fared almost as badly. They were able to get a better look at her bonnet, dress, petticoats, and other voluminous underclothing which up to that time she had not discarded.

The customs men were a little disappointed, for they found nothing concealed even among the many petticoats; so only a very small bribe could be demanded. Then the Judsons were allowed to dress and proceed to what Ann called "the largest and handsomest house in all Rangoon." This was the mission home of Felix Carey and his Burmese-born wife, a woman of Portuguese descent who, although she could speak little English, gave the weary travelers a very warm welcome. Felix himself had been ordered by the King to go to the Golden City of Ava where several little princes and princesses needed vaccination.

Mrs. Carey was kindness itself. She did her best to make the American couple feel at home in their new surroundings, introducing them to such strange foods as fowls stewed with cucumbers, curried rice and curried fowl. The Burmese way of life was quite different even from that of India.

In Burma the slaughter of animals for food was not allowed. Only those animals that had died natural or accidental deaths could lawfully be eaten.

The first few days were spent in exploring their immediate surroundings. They discovered that there was no caste system as in India and in spite of corruption in high places the Burmese possessed an indomitable spirit of independence. Their greatest fault was telling lies. "We cannot live without telling lies," they told Ann, who was a little taken back at finding lying so common among them.

Life in the bazaars provided a never-ending source of amusement to the Judsons. The women, and even small babies, chewed betel, a narcotic stimulant made by slicing the nut of the areca palm. In time it turned teeth black and lips scarlet.

The men, who tattooed their smooth brown bodies with blue dye, wore patsos or waistcloths. Each patso contained eight yards of brilliant silk, sometimes patterned with checks or stripes. As there were no banks, the people wore their wealth on their own persons. Huge holes were bored through their earlobes, into which they pushed golden pellets. If the owner were very rich, precious stones adorned these "earplugs." Those with no gold used their hollowed ear lobes for convenient cigar holders!

Soon after their arrival Adoniram and Ann visited the famed Shwe-Dagon Pagoda, located on the highest hill in Rangoon. Buddhist teachings relate that the Lord Buddha was asked by some of his followers to tell them how they might show their devotion to him. The Buddha then spread out his square cloak on the ground, turned his alms bowl upside down and held his staff above the bowl, thus intimating the shape in which he wished a pagoda to be built. The original Shwe-Dagon was built soon after the death of the Buddha. Through the centuries it was enlarged and beautified by successive generations of his faithful followers until its golden spire reached the impressive height of three hundred and sixty-eight feet. Burmese merchants brought relics of the Lord Buddha's hair to be enshrined in the great pagoda.

It was necessary to remove their footwear before ascending one of the four stairways leading on to the sacred platform. Ann's strong New England leather boots and her husband's buckled shoes made strange companions beside the flimsy Burmese sandals. Giant chinthe lions and grim-looking sculptures of mythical ogres guarded the entrances while halfway up the sloping ground a pathway ran round the hill where worshippers could walk to recite a cycle-like prayer. Here it seemed they were standing in the very heart of Burma.

Ann held tightly to Adoniram's arm as they peeped into the arcades and openings filled with small shrines holding rich, stone-studded figures of the Buddha. Close by were open-sided *zayats* where monks sat in their saffron robes, either meditating or leading others in prayer.

Nobody bothered the foreign visitors, who were free to

explore every niche and cranny. Pretty Burmese women with flowers in their hair came bearing gifts of food and flowers to place before a favorite statue of the Buddha, first touching their heads to the ground in reverent obeisance. Sometimes they bought tiny tins of water from the ever-present water carrier, to pour over the Buddha's head. The rich would purchase packages of gold leaf and then make their way to the dome where they would carefully "anoint" its already gold-covered surface.

Walking unshod around the great platform, the Judsons saw the five hundred golden *stupas* representing the five hundred chief disciples who followed the Buddha during his earthly lifetime, and listened as the golden bells of the *hti* (spire) tinkled in the soft, balmy wind. As they listened they must have thought of those other bells that rang from the narrow steeples of the white New England churches so many thousands of miles away. Perhaps they felt a stab of homesickness, for up to then they had not received one letter from their families. It was two and a half years after leaving Salem that the first long-anticipated letters arrived.

But the Judsons had not come to Burma for sight-seeing; they had come to bring the message of the Christian Gospel. First the difficult language had to be mastered, so a teacher must be found. Ann was just as keen as Adoniram to learn Burmese, as the European wives spoke French, a language of which she could speak only a few words. She complained, "There is no female in all Burma with whom I can converse."

At last an instructor was engaged, but the prospect of teaching a woman made him very unhappy. Discussing his feelings, Ann writes of the new teacher as "appearing to feel that it was rather beneath him to instruct a female, as the females here are held in the lowest estimation. But when he saw I was determined to persevere, and that Mr. Judson was desirous that he should instruct me as himself, he was more attentive."

The man agreed to teach them but then came the snag. He could not speak English and they knew no Burmese. All they could do was to sit on their individual mats smiling helplessly at one another before Adoniram hit on a simple yet effective plan. He would point to something in the room, giving its English name. The teacher would then pronounce the Burmese equivalent. It was hard going even though they studied for twelve hours each day.

In place of paper the teacher used palm leaves for writing. The circles and half-circles were easy enough to copy but reading was another matter, for there was no visible punctuation or even the usual separation between each word. It was grinding work and in their own minds they seemed to progress but little, although their teacher was very pleased with them. He even told Ann that he was going to *her* land when he died, which for a Burmese was a great compliment.

After nearly five months of intensive studying Adoniram thought he knew enough basic everyday phrases to call on Mya-day-men, the viceroy and ruler of the city. They must win the friendship of this man who was empowered to kill anybody on a whim. Poor Adoniram was most disappointed by his reception, and, annoyed by her husband's treatment, Ann wrote in her journal that the ruler "scarcely deigned to look at him, as Englishmen are no uncommon sight in this country." Then she had an idea. Adoniram might be quite ordinary to the Burmese eye but she was *extraordinary*— even "quite a curiosity." She put on her scoop bonnet, chose a small present to take with her and, accompanied by a friendly woman married to a Frenchman, set off to visit the head-wife at Government House.

When they arrived they found that lady to be still in bed,

and so they had to wait. The viceroy's lesser wives were delighted. One by one they came up to examine every small detail of the visitors' gloves, bonnets and gowns. Tittering and laughing at what they found, they voiced their opinions in rather loud voices. Suddenly a deep silence fell over the reception room; the extra wives retired quietly to a far corner. The head-wife had arrived.

Brilliantly attired and smoking a long silver pipe, she apologized for being late by saying she was not well. Then leading Ann by the hand to a mat she motioned that she should sit down beside her. This was the signal for a woman to appear with a bunch of flowers, with which the head-wife decorated not only her own cap but her visitor's scoop bonnet as well. Ann, feeling quite at ease, smiled with delight. Then the viceroy's wife started to question her. "Are you your husband's first wife?"—meaning was she the head-wife. Ann tactfully replied that she was. She did not want to offend the other woman by saying that unlike the Burmese, Americans were allowed only one wife at a time. She was then asked if she intended to stay long in the country. Before she could answer there was a rustling of robes and Ann looked up to be confronted by a man whom she described after this first meeting as "a savage-looking creature." Probably any other woman would have thought the same; he was carrying an enormous spear. His outsize *patso* was knotted up in front of his legs like a pair of trousers.

Ann managed to conceal her true feelings and even muster a smile. This pleased the viceroy so much that he spoke very kindly to her, asking if she would like a cup of rum. She courteously declined, being a minister's wife and an abstainer. Mya-day-men, satisfied, bowed low before stamping out.

At last it was time to go; the audience was over. The

head-wife took Ann's hand in her own. "You are like a sister to me," she announced rather surprisingly, and paid Ann the great compliment of accompanying her to the door.

Mrs. Adoniram Judson's visit had been an unprecedented success.

nine

"T hey are just cut out for this mission. I thought so, as soon as I first met them. In six months Mr. Judson has a splendid grasp of the language, and is the very colleague I wanted."

So wrote Felix Carey from the mission house just outside the city walls of Rangoon to his father, Dean William Carey. Perhaps he wrote with some sense of relief at having found two such enthusiastic young people as the Judsons to carry on the missionary work which he was about to give up. Felix had been offered an important government post at the court of King Bodawpaya in the Golden City of Ava. Before accepting he felt duty bound to visit his father and explain the reasons for wanting to take on the new and difficult task at the Burmese court.

He had not been gone long when the Judsons decided it would be wise to live in a house within the city walls. Bands of robbers were roaming the countryside and they deemed the city a safer place in which to live. Besides, they would get to know the inhabitants better if they lived amongst them instead of in the rather isolated mission house.

During the early part of January 1814 they moved, and none too soon, for shortly afterwards robbers attacked and pillaged a home close to the mission, killing the owner.

They were now becoming used to the day-by-day excitement of living in a Burmese city. Even the steamy heat and mixture of smells no longer bothered them. One day they attended the funeral of a rich Burmese which greatly intrigued them. There was a long parade of elephants of various sizes, some covered with rich trappings, while at the actual cremation pyre gifts of money and food were distributed to the eager crowd of mourners. The excitement did not end there, for on the way home an assassin leapt upon a local governor and with one sweep of his sword beheaded him.

Ann's stomach was beginning to get used to such sudden shocks. She calmly tells us that the murderer was identified as being the governor's chief steward; that after killing his master he planned upon seizing his possessions. He also intended to go to King Bodawpaya and purchase the governor's office for himself. After being tortured, the assassin lived only a few days. Ann notes that "the immense property of this governor goes to the king, as he left no children, although several wives remain." She felt rather sorry for these unfortunate multiple widows.

On another happier occasion they joined the jostling crowd to cheer a baby white elephant who with its gray mother had been discovered in the jungle.

One Sunday in March the Judsons decided to take a walk out to the mission house to visit Mrs. Carey, who, already the mother of a three-year-old boy, now had another baby. They had hardly arrived when a frightened servant burst into the room with the news that a fire had broken out near the town. Hurrying to the scene the Judsons found several houses ablaze, with the flames spreading rapidly toward the city proper. They were amazed that nobody was trying to put the fire out. In no time, they decided, the whole of Rangoon would be a burning holocaust.

Hurrying to the town gates, they were further horrified to find them locked, for although they were made of wood, the inhabitants firmly believed that by closing them they would shut out the fire. It was only after much pleading that they were opened and the Judsons allowed through. As quickly as possible they took their few possessions from the town house back to the mission, where Mrs. Carey once more received them with kindness.

On her husband's return from Calcutta she set out with him by water for Ava. A few miles distant from Rangoon a sudden storm arose, overturning their boat. Felix Carey had the terrible experience of seeing his wife, small son and new baby drown before his eyes. The news did not reach the Judsons, now left to their own devices in the mission house, until two weeks afterwards.

Felix, suffering from shock, was slow to recover from the loss of his wife and little ones and for four years was somewhat "eccentric." He appeared at Calcutta in the self-styled role of Burma's ambassador to the British Government, entering the city with gold sword, gold and ivory handled scarlet silk umbrella and fifty suitably attired Burmese attendants. The government had already provided him with a mansion when suddenly it was discovered that he had defective credentials. Whether this was due to negligence on the part of the King of Burma's secretary at Ava or to Felix's having exaggerated the nature of his mission is not clear. However, Felix stayed on in Calcutta for several months accruing debts that his father William Carey honored. It was a time of painful humiliation and personal suffering to the elder Carey, who said of the episode, "It is very distressing to be forced to apologize for those you love." To another son, Jabez, he wrote, "Felix's drifting from God has nearly broken my heart."

At length Felix returned to Burma but, hearing of the King's moodiness and fearing his anger, fled. Of these sad years S. Pearce Carey, in his biography, *William Carey*, writes,

For three years he (Felix) roamed over the frontier-borders between Burmah and Assam—exploring, botanizing, learning vernaculars, serving the Raja of Cachar, gathering and transmitting to Calcutta political information of the much-agitated tribes and peoples, and once even captaining a little force against hopelessly-outnumbering Burmese raiders. Throughout the three years he kept in touch with his father, whose letters, he said, 'cheered my soul.' At length, at the end of 1818, met by good hap near Chittagong by Ward [the Reverend William Ward, missionary colleague of the senior Carey and the man who had baptized Adoniram and Ann], his tenderhearted spiritual father, he was constrained back to 'Serampore,' to the solace of them all. With his dear prodigal home again, Carey could 'begin to be merry.'

Felix died towards the end of 1822 from fever, his father outliving him.

For the first time since their marriage Ann and Adoniram could really boast of a home of their very own if one did not count the short-lived venture in the tiny town house that had been destroyed by fire. While Adoniram spent his mornings with the Burmese teacher Ann was obliged to devote hers to dealing with the various servants connected with the mission. These household tasks were not without their own reward, for after a year Ann found that her daily contact with the servants had given her a better command of the spoken language than her husband had acquired in the same time from his teacher. Although somewhat envious of her vocabulary, Adoniram consoled himself with the knowledge that his own studies would eventually result in a Burmese Bible. He was also compiling a grammar and the material for a dictionary.

Day after day the Burmese teacher, a dignified man of sixty with a spotlessly clean white cloth tied about his head, arrived to instruct Adoniram. As she went about her own work Ann could hear the steady hum of their voices.

Life in a Rangoon home was at times hard for the missionary wife from Massachusetts. Cockroaches, bedbugs, beetles, bats and spiders were only a few of the pests that had to be dealt with. Ann even dealt with an unwelcome cobra in the mission compound! The spiders, large as a man's fist, though dreadful to look at, were really very cowardly. They would spring at her bare arms but never actually strike.

With the ingenuity of a true New England housewife she had added variety to the spicy but monotonous Burmese fare of curried fowl, rice and vegetables. She learned to churn butter from the poor-grade milk, made preserves and pies from the native fruits growing in the garden and invented an alternative to flour by pounding together banana-like plantains and ordinary rice. She even invented a custard! Real flour, sugar and tea could be ordered from Bengal.

Keeping themselves clean was no problem. The city possessed a number of artificial ponds pleasantly shaded with trees. The Europeans called these "tanks." The Judsons found bathing in them very refreshing.

They were also making friends. The Burmese would pay evening calls, bringing little gifts. The unpopular viceroy Mya-day-men who had offered Ann a cup of rum had left the city. His successor was an elderly man with many wives and over a score of children. He came in person to visit the mission, where his head-wife immediately took to Ann. One day at a special party given in Government House for the Europeans living in the city the new viceroy's wife decided to honor Mrs. Judson by asking her to dance for the guests. Ann must have recalled the old happy days of dancing in the frolic room at Bradford with the other youngsters but that was all in the past. Besides she had no wish to create a bad impression. Smiling at her hostess she explained that the wife of a "priest" could not dance as it would be improper. Her regal friend understood; after all, holy people even in Burma had their own special rules for living.

Eighteen months after their arrival in Rangoon Ann started to loose weight. Each day she seemed to grow weaker and although Adoniram diligently searched the few medical books they possessed he could find no illness comparable to his wife's. Actually she was suffering from the type of wasting disease then common in the Far East. This was not the only problem; Ann believed she might be pregnant again.

The nearest European doctor was in Madras; Ann would have to make the journey. Adoniram was anxious to go with her but she absolutely refused his offer. His studies were important. She insisted it was better that he should stay behind in Rangoon.

Remembering their dreadful voyage on the crazy old

Georgiana and his wife's confinement on the open deck he determined that whatever happened she must not travel alone. Surely a Burmese woman could accompany her in case an emergency should arise. However there existed a rigid law forbidding any Burmese woman to leave her native land.

Then they thought of the kindly old viceroy and his friendly head-wife. Taking a small gift, which was the custom when one was asking a special favor, the Judsons presented themselves at Government House with their request. The governor immediately ordered an official permit to be given allowing the Burmese woman to travel with Ann. Not only that; he insisted on covering the expense of her passage.

Late in January of 1815 Ann set sail with her Burmese helper, safely reaching Madras where after a stay of six weeks she was noticeably better. The chance to renew old acquaintances acted like an additional tonic, while they in turn were amazed by all she had to tell of life in Burma, a country to which, on her former visit, they were so firmly against her traveling. One young man who had been particularly kind to the Judsons and other Christian workers was a Mr. Van Someren, son of a major in the Dutch army, who made it his business to visit the ships lying in the Madras roads, claiming the arriving missionaries as his own guests. They were taken to his large roomy house, entertained, advised upon business interests and then sent with godspeed on their journey. He was the guardian of three young cousins who had been orphaned. Ann became very attached to the youngest of these, a child named Emily Van Someren, longing to take her back to Burma. Van Someren, impressed with Mrs. Judson's character and charm, consented. Ann in turn promised to raise her as one of the family.

The voyage back to Rangoon went very smoothly. Ann could hardly wait for the ship to dock, so impatient was she to tell Adoniram that all was well. He also had to make the acquaintance of Emily.

During her absence he had quietly continued his studies, but so far he had been unable to convert a single Burmese to Christianity. A son of the viceroy did at one time show interest in the new religion but unfortunately his father was replaced by the same spear-stalking Mya-day-men he had succeeded. With his proud position gone, the old viceroy's son also seemed to lose his sense of dignity and in addition his interest in Adoniram's teachings.

Physically tired but mentally undaunted, Adoniram decided that the more he mastered the Burmese language the better would be his chance of attracting converts. Ann did her best to help him by approaching the womenfolk, but always the answer was the same: "Your religion is good for you, ours for us. You will be rewarded for your good deeds in your way—we in our way."

September 5, 1815, was a memorable day in the life of the Judsons, for letters arrived at last from America. They had been without direct news from their homeland since leaving the Isle of France two years before. The important information—apart from the more personal letters received from members of the Judson and Hasseltine families—was the reaction of the Baptists in New England to the baptism of Adoniram and Ann. Immediately they had set out to organize local societies whose object would be the support of the new missionaries. Luther Rice, who had been among the five young men (Adoniram included) to be ordained missionaries at Tabernacle Church, Haverhill, on that memorable night of February 6, 1812, was responsible for the birth of Baptist missionary societies in almost every state in

100

the Union. Rice, like Adoniram, had undergone a change of denomination from Congregationalist to Baptist and had also been baptized in India. Because of recurring liver trouble he had been unable to pursue an active career in the mission field, deciding instead to return to the United States where, while undergoing treatment for his condition, he could work on the promotion of a Baptist missionary enterprise.

During the month of May, 1814, "The General Missionary Convention of the Baptist Denomination in the United States of America for Foreign Missions" was formed with headquarters in Philadelphia. The Reverend Thomas Baldwin of Boston was made President of the newly elected Board of Managers while the Reverend Dr. William Staughton of Philadelphia became the Corresponding Secretary. Adoniram was appointed by the new Board as its missionary.

On September 11 Ann gave birth to a little boy. Once more her husband was both doctor and nurse. The baby, who had blue eyes, was named after Roger Williams, Puritan clergyman and founder of the colony of Rhode Island where he died in 1683. Two weeks after the birth Ann felt well enough to write her mother that "since the birth of our little son my health has been much better than for two years before. I feel now almost in a new state of existence."

Little Emily was also doing well in her new surroundings. As was only childlike, she picked up everyday Burmese words and sentences with ease. Life in the mission house at Rangoon at this period in the Judsons' lives was very pleasant indeed.

ten

There had never been such an interesting baby in Rangoon as Roger Williams Judson; at least it seemed that way. Even the viceroy's head-wife was delighted when Ann took him to show her.

"What a child; How white!" she repeated again and again. Roger was placed on the rich velvet cushion which was usually reserved for the vicereine herself. Then she sat down and played with him. From the beginning Roger had been a responsive child. He enjoyed being with people and would lie for hours on the mat by his father's study table.

The vicereine enjoyed herself very much; in fact she played with the baby so long that his mother was afraid they were overstaying their welcome. The vicereine shook her head. They must remain so that her husband could view the wonder child. Eventually the fierce Mya-day-men marched into the room, as usual carrying his long spear.

"Look, my lord, see what a child! Look at his feet! Look at his hands!" The viceroy laughed aloud. He was just as delighted over Roger as his wife had been. He carefully examined the baby's fat little arms and legs, congratulated his proud mother and again offered her a cup of rum, which even on this special occasion she respectfully declined. At last she was allowed to take Roger home.

For six wonderful months Roger was their joy. He seldom cried, regularly gained weight and seemed in every respect a normal, healthy child. Then early in March he began to show signs of fever; during the nighttime the little fellow was covered with sweat, filling his parents with alarm. In vain did the kindly Burmese women tell them that all would be well when he had cut his first teeth.

In addition Adoniram himself was far from well. The strain of so much concentrated studying was beginning to tell. At times he felt too weak even to stand; his eyes burned so much that he could no longer read or even see properly to write. Worried that the mission was ended before it had hardly begun, harassed by frantic fears over the baby's sickness, Adoniram spent hours of utter misery wondering what could be done. Not since the time he had been taken captive by the French privateer and thrown into the dirty, evil-smelling hold had he felt so depressed.

Early one May morning while Ann was lifting Roger from his cradle he was taken with a terrible fit of coughing which continued for half an hour. More fever followed. Next day Roger's heavy breathing could be heard all over the mission house. There was no doctor in the city. The only man with any knowledge of medicine was a Portuguese priest who immediately answered their cry for help. He prescribed a small quantity of rhubarb and gascoign powder, but it seemed to have little effect. Two nights later the baby died. Ann poignantly recorded the tragedy in her journal: "He [Adoniram] laid him in his cradle—he slept with ease for half-an-hour, when his breath stopped without a struggle, and he was gone! Thus died our little Roger."

Following is the verse:

> 'Short pain, short grief, dear babe, was thine—
> Now, joys eternal and divine.'

The young parents were absolutely numb with sorrow. This was the second child they had lost and although Ann's own sense of pain was overwhelming it was made even more so by the terrible grief of Adoniram. Her generous heart was filled with compassion for him.

Because of the climate the funeral was held a few hours afterwards. Roger, the first child to be born of white parents in Burma in living memory, was buried in an enclosure of mango trees in the mission house garden near the bamboo hut where his mother had so often sat to pen her frequent letters home. Now all they had left were a few crude toys and a cradle. The suddenness of their bereavement made it all the more difficult to comprehend. For a week they wanted to see nobody while all the time their eyes would wander to the fresh mound in the garden. Then one day they heard a great noise in the mission house compound. Everywhere they looked there seemed to be people. At last they recognized Mya-day-men's wife, the vicereine. She had been told of the little white child's death only that day and was very affected by the news. Smiting her breast in the Burmese expression of grief, she cried in a loud voice, "Why did you not send me word, that I might have come to his funeral?"

The parents were deeply touched, Ann explaining that in their sudden and great sorrow the thought had not occurred to them. The vicereine nodded her head in understanding, begging them to be brave, particularly telling Adoniram to take care of his own health. Ann, feeling better already for another woman's comfort, quickly prepared refreshments. She set out sweetmeats, little cakes, green tea and ginger for the very distinguished mourner.

A few days later they received a further communication from the vicereine. She had thought long over their troubles, coming to the conclusion that they both needed a change of scene. In memory of the little white child she was arranging a procession of elephants. A conveyance would be sent to fetch them at the appropriate time.

It was! A large elephant with a beautifully draped *howdah* (seat) strapped to its back arrived, complete with driver. In time the huge beast with the Judsons seated on it joined the rest of the parade. They had never seen such a procession. The vicereine, dressed in a brilliant gown of white and red silk, rode ahead of the Judsons' elephant. Her beast was a little larger than theirs and the *howdah* in which she sat was covered with gilt that glittered in the bright morning sunshine. The procession was led into the jungle by a guard of thirty red-capped men carrying either spears or guns. Behind the Judsons' elephant were three or four more of the large beasts bearing the viceroy's son and important government officials. Following on foot were some three hundred brightly attired men and women.

The journey lay through cool, thick jungle, so overgrown in places with bamboo strands and coarse elephant grass that the elephants themselves were needed to clear a passageway through. Huge teak trees, sometimes towering one

106

hundred and twenty feet above the ground, cast their long shadows on brilliant orchids, strange wild fruits and hanging vines. Butterflies and moths of every conceivable color darted in search of the sunlight over the heads of the intruders. Monkeys chattered unceasingly as they disappeared into the waiting branches. Once the Judsons caught sight of a python, its slick shiny body curled round the trunk of a tree, sleeping so soundly that even the crashing din made by the elephants failed to disturb it. Ann and Adoniram were amused when a herd of young deer barking like dogs sprang into the high grass and were immediately lost to view.

At last the vicereine signaled for the procession to halt under a spreading banyan tree whose branches had sent out hanging roots which on reaching the ground themselves made other trees. Mats were unrolled so that the guests of honor might sit with their regal hostess, who did all in her power to make them happy. With her own hands she twisted garlands of blossoms for her American friends. Then, gathering fruit, she herself pared it as a mark of condescension and devotion.

It was already dark before the elephant set them down in front of the mission house. Tired out, their hearts full of gratitude, Adoniram and Ann went indoors to spend their most relaxed night since the death of their little one. The elephant party given by the vicereine had worked its own soothing therapy upon them.

eleven

Ann's grief for the loss of Roger was eased a little by the presence of the Dutch girl, Emily Van Someren, in the mission house. In an effort to forget, she quickly organized a small school for girls and was also hard at work writing a simple catechism in Burmese. In no time she had thirty pupils whose mothers would often sit in on the lessons. It gave her a wonderful opportunity of getting to know more Burmese women, to whom she tried to tell something of Christianity. When she was not teaching or keeping house she spent her time translating the Book of Jonah into Burmese. It may seem rather a strange choice but one must remember that Ann was a New Englander who had grown up with the stirring exploits of the whaling ships ringing in her ears.

Adoniram's eyes were still troubling him. They burned so much that at times he could scarcely see at all. A visiting sea captain suggested horse-riding as a form of exercise which might help them and at the same time clear up his terrible headaches.

During the month of October, 1816, something wonderful happened that made the Judsons rejoice. George H. Hough, a new missionary recently accepted by the Baptist Board of Managers with his wife Phebe, arrived via Calcutta from America with their two children *and a printing press.* Hough was to print whatever the Judsons had written or translated into Burmese. Adoniram was delighted, for he was sure that once the King in Ava heard of the wondrous new press he would want to see it work for himself.

The Houghs, a pleasant couple, were quite happy sharing the mission house with the Judsons. Phebe immediately began to learn how to run a Burmese home while her husband set up the precious press. The first seven-page tract that he printed was one Adoniram had completed when feeling so sick that he thought he would have to abandon his missionary calling. It included the story of Adam and Eve and the Commandments, and finished with the following Burmese touch:

In the year of Christ, 1816; in the Burman year, 1178; in the 967th day of the lord of the Saddan elephant, and master of the Sakyah weapon; and in the 33rd year of his reign; in the division Pashoo; on Tuesday, the 12th day of the wane of the moon Wahgoung, after the double beat, this writing, entitled *The Way to Heaven,* was finished. *May the reader obtain light.* Amen.

Hough's next assignment was to set Ann's catechism, which he did by matching the sausagelike strings of circles in type, although their meaning he did not understand. It was entitled *Mrs. Judson's Catechism.*

He then started work on Adoniram's translation of the Gospel according to St. Matthew. The missionary wished he could translate as quickly as Hough could print!

A few Burmese requested copies of the "holy books," as they called the new printings. Ann's school flourished. Her good friend the vicereine even consented to talk with her "privately" on the subject of religion, allowing one of her own daughters to read Ann's catechism. Adoniram's sore eyes and headaches were somewhat better, though he could not say if the horse riding prescribed by the sea captain was the reason. Undaunted, he had already started work on a Burmese dictionary. He believed future missionaries to Burma would find his grammar and dictionary invaluable. Yet even after so much effort, the hard fact remained that the mission still could not boast a single convert.

Then one night during Tabaung, the last month of the Burmese year, which is March in the western world, something exciting happened. A well-dressed man attended by his servant arrived at the mission house and promptly seated himself on the mat beside Adoniram.

"How long will it take me to learn the religion of Jesus?" was his somewhat startling greeting.

Adoniram quietly replied, "Such a question cannot be answered. If God gives light and wisdom, the religion of Jesus is soon learned. Without God, a man may study all his life long and make no progress."

When asked if he had seen any writings concerning Jesus, the Burmese, whose name was Maung Yah, answered, "He is the Son of God, who, pitying human creatures, came into this world and suffered death in their stead."

Rather taken back by the visitor's knowledge, Adoniram

111

handed him a copy of Ann's little catechism, together with his own tract. The Burmese smiled. *He had seen them before.* After reading aloud from each in turn he then declared to his servant, "This is the true God. This is the right way."

Adoniram was filled with gratitude, for he knew without doubt that their printed efforts were beginning to bear good fruit. Before Maung Yah left the mission he had also been presented with the first five printed chapters of Matthew.

Ann, with the exception of her footwear, now dressed like a Burmese woman. Somehow she could never get used to open sandals. By New England standards of the early eighteen hundreds her mode of attire would appear to be somewhat immodest, perhaps even daring, yet it suited her tall, well-developed figure very well. From the waist up she wore a blouselike garment of black lace or yellow gauze known as an *aingyi,* while her *longyi* or shirt made of brilliant flowered silk was gathered in folds at the breast.

Adoniram still clung to his funereal black suits but did not object at all to his wife's copying Burmese dress. The fashion-conscious Burmese women considered it a compliment that 'the teacher's' wife should imitate them.

Now, in addition to her school, Ann was holding Sunday meetings for women. Although listening politely as she discussed her own religion, they admitted with native frankness at the end of each session that they had no desire to give up their Buddhist faith. Even Ann had to smile when one woman confessed she would rather spend eternity in hell with her own family and ancestors than in heaven with a lot of people she didn't know.

Meanwhile Maung Yah, the Burmese who called to ask

112

about Jesus, had not returned. George Hough thought that neither the Judsons nor he would live to see a Burmese baptized, but Adoniram felt differently. Surely in time they would get one convert. In Chittagong, Bengal, less than two weeks' sailing time from Rangoon, he had heard that there were Christians who formerly had lived under Burmese rule. These Christians, who had been converted by a Baptist mission, belonged to a group of natives known as Mugs. If he could go there and persuade some of them to return with him to Rangoon, other Burmese, seeing that Christianity was not just a foreigner's religion, might be tempted to embrace it. The more often the Judsons and Houghs thought about Chittagong, the more it seemed a practical solution in their tantalizing search for converts.

Once Adoniram or his equally persistent wife had an idea, there was no stopping them from trying to carry it out. Consequently on Christmas Eve, 1817, Adoniram boarded the ship *Two Brothers* en route for Chittagong.

For a few weeks after his departure things continued in a normal manner. The vicereine had taken Ann for more elephant rides, while Maung Yah, the man who inquired about Jesus, had returned. Having been made governor in the Pegu country, east of Rangoon, he had been unable to come before. Now he wanted more books.

Ann had inquired tactfully if he were yet ready to become a Christian, to which question he replied encouragingly, "Not yet, but I am thinking and reading in order to become one. But I cannot destroy my old mind. When I see a handsome waistcloth or turban I still desire it. Tell the great teacher when he returns that I wish to see him, though I am not yet a disciple of Christ."

Encouraged at least by his frankness, Ann had presented him with the rest of Adoniram's translation of St. Matthew. Maung Yah was very touched, explaining that he now governed a thousand homes. Would they not visit him, he suggested, and he would arrange a congregation of his people to hear the teacher preach.

During March, Mya-day-men the viceroy and his gracious wife were ordered back to Ava. His successor arrived alone in Rangoon. This was difficult for Ann because a woman could not visit the governor's home unless he had a wife there to receive her. Burmese protocol, which the Judsons were always careful to respect, forbade it.

They had hardly left Rangoon when a native ship arrived from Chittagong with the startling news that the *Two Brothers* had never reached its destination. Though Ann was perfectly aware that ships were often blown off course in the treacherous Bay, she had further cause to worry when friends from Bengal itself wrote her that nowhere in their vicinity had they heard of the *Two Brothers* landing.

Had the ship with her husband on board been lost at sea? Ann Judson refused to believe that it had.

Shortly afterwards George Hough had been ordered to appear at the courthouse. Obeying the summons at once, he was told by the officials that if he did not explain his purpose for coming to Burma "they would write with his heart's blood." Hough was a pleasant man but he was only a printer. He did not have either Adoniram's or Ann's natural gifts for leadership or oratory. He could not even appeal personally to the new viceroy because unlike the missionaries he did not speak fluent Burmese. At the courthouse he underwent a long period of interrogation, during which

114

time he was not allowed to leave the room for any purpose at all. He was asked thousands of questions, some so trivial that he could not understand why they should be asked.

"How many suits of clothing do you possess?"

"What are the names of your parents?"

Poor George Hough sweated and fidgeted, which seemed only to delight his tormentors the more. Slowly, methodically, they wrote down his answers on dried palm leaves. He was refused food or water.

At the mission house Mrs. Hough was in a state bordering on hysteria, with her young children clinging to her long skirts. She was sure she would never see her husband again. Ann, putting aside her own fears that Adoniram might be drowned at sea, managed to keep calm. She had lived among the Burmese long enough to suspect that there was a hidden reason behind this sudden relentless persecution of the insignificant George Hough. She even wondered if the new viceroy knew anything of the questioning. Were the dishonest courthouse officials acting without the viceroy's knowledge in order to obtain a large bribe for their own pockets?

Hough had only just been released when another order arrived, demanding his attendance at Court on a Sunday. This was too much for Mrs. Judson's New England scruples. Armed with a written petition explaining Hough's case, emphasizing that he had been ordered to make a public appearance "on our sacred day," protocol or not, Ann accompanied the unhappy printer to the doors of Government House itself.

The sight of a white woman waving a petition in the crowded courtyard was soon brought to the attention of the viceroy, who immediately sent a secretary to read its message. Then his voice, known as "the voice which issues life

115

or death," inquired angrily, "Why has the examination of this foreign teacher been prolonged in this way?"

When Ann finally left Government House she had the viceroy's assurance that the printer, who was allowed to go home, would be questioned no more—and certainly not on a Sunday. But her triumph was short-lived, for many Burmese, seeing that the foreigners were "not as important" as they had hitherto thought them, decided the mission house was hardly worth visiting. Ann's Sunday meetings for the women suffered, their attendances dwindling to a mere handful.

Then a terrible plague struck Rangoon. Although common in India, there had never been an epidemic of cholera in Burma before, and the population was panic-stricken. People died by the hundreds. With the disease occurring during the hottest season of the year, a man could be perfectly fit in the morning and dead by nightfall.

Day after day the inhabitants of Rangoon beat upon their houses with clubs, for they were sure evil spirits were wandering through the city killing off its people. The only thing to keep such spirits at bay was to make as much noise as possible. Heavy cannon fire from the courthouse inaugurated the initial uproar. Day and night the din continued. There was nothing to do but wait and pray. It seemed a miracle that at the mission nobody sickened with cholera.

The epidemic actually continued until the start of the rainy season. Already hard set by the plague, the people of Rangoon were further harassed by the rumor that the British were planning to invade the country. There seemed some truth in the story, for no British ships had docked in Rangoon for months.

For a number of years, ever since the Burmese King had plundered his own rebellious borderlands, causing the inhabitants to flee into British territories nearby, there had been frequent rumors of war. From time to time he had crossed the border in an effort to force the refugees back into Burma. There were skirmishes with British outposts, resulting in damage to life and property. The British, fully occupied in India, did not hasten to deal with the Burmese intruders, who mistook their apparent indifference for cowardice. Now it seemed possible that they were about to retaliate.

Poor George Hough; arrest, cholera and now war. He had never been happy in Burma—was still unable to master the language properly or see any possible conversion of the Burmese to Christianity. As for Judson, he must be dead. Hough decided there was no alternative but to pack up and return to Calcutta. After all, as he explained to Ann, anything that needed to be printed in Burmese could just as well be printed there in safety. He begged her to go too but she refused.

Ann still could not believe that her husband was dead. He might yet sail up the river to Rangoon, expecting her to be waiting so that they might continue their chosen life work together.

Night after night she heard the pounding of clubs, the hollow beating of drums and roaring of cannon, for cholera still raged. At times she nearly went mad with worry. A ship for India lay in the river with the Houghs already aboard. In a fit of depression Ann decided to join them. She paid her passage, said good-by to her servants and joined the ship with Emily. With heavy heart she watched as the anchor was raised and they drifted slowly down the river. Had she done right? What would happen if war with the British did come? Even if she heard that her husband was safe and had somehow got back to Rangoon,

117

the port would be closed and she unable to join him. This distressing thought turned over and over in her mind. Further down-river the ship made its last call to collect cargo, at which time Mrs. Judson took advantage of a woman's prerogative to change her mind. Ordering her baggage off the ship, she hired a small boat and returned to Rangoon. The Burmese left in the plague-imprisoned mission house greeted the return of the teacher's wife as a good omen. War, plague or anything else, Ann Judson was there to stay.

Then one day while working at her studies she was interrupted by the news that the *Two Brothers* had arrived back at Rangoon. Throwing down her books, she ran to the wharf and sought out the captain. Adoniram, she learned, was alive in Madras. Overjoyed with the news, she slowly retraced her steps to the mission house where she sought out little Emily. Hand in hand they entered the grove of mangrove trees where Roger was buried. Then, falling on her knees, she began to cry. This time her tears were not those of sorrow for her lost baby, but of sheer relief at Adoniram's safety.

Ten days later the Houghs were back in Rangoon, their sailing delayed. At last came the most wonderful moment of all. A ship was coming up the river. His ship. Adoniram Judson was at last coming home.

"What happened?" Ann and Adoniram breathlessly asked the same question when finally the ship landed and they were safe at last in each other's arms. As soon as the usual long customs proceedings were over they hurried home to the mission house where Adoniram listened first to his wife's incredible story about Hough's arrest before telling his own.

As it turned out, his much-anticipated trip to the territory of the Baptist converts had been one long nightmare; for hardly were they at sea when his eye trouble and headaches returned with a vengeance. He took to his bunk in agony. This was not all, for, running into strong head winds, the ship was blown completely off course. Reluctantly her captain gave up hopes of reaching Chittagong, setting a new course for Madras. Adoniram was furious, for he had no wish to visit unfriendly India. However, the *Two Brothers* was unable to make Madras either, trying instead for Masulipatam, north of Madras. Day after day the ship floundered hopelessly in the Bay of Bengal, while down in his cabin Adoniram, deathly ill, was fighting a raging fever. Water had run out; sometimes they passed a native boat whose crew would generously give them a bucket or two, which naturally had to be rationed. Adoniram was burning up. Hungry, dirty—for he had brought clothing to last two weeks, not two months—he was all but dead when three months after leaving Rangoon the ship finally anchored in the mud some miles from Masulipatam.

Miraculously he managed to write a few words begging that "any English resident of Masulipatam" would allow him a place to die on dry land. Shortly afterwards through the porthole he glimpsed a small boat loaded with red-coated British soldiers and civilians. Shocked by his appearance, they promptly took him ashore to the home of a British officer who did everything possible to make him well.

In time his eyes did not burn so much; the headaches gradually ceased. Finding that the *Two Brothers* could not return to Rangoon for several months, his only alternative was to go to Madras, three hundred miles away, where there might possibly be a ship ready to sail there. A hundred times during his illness his thoughts had strayed to Ann and the Mission. He abandoned all hope of ever getting to Chittagong. The most sensible course was to return to Rangoon as speedily as possible; so, hiring a *palanquin* and bearers, he made the long journey overland, arriving in Madras on April 8, only to meet another disappointment, for no ship was sailing to Rangoon for several months. It was not until July that one did.

twelve

Weeks passed and the Houghs were still in the mission house. Adoniram did his best to persuade them to stay but to no avail. As soon as their ship could sail they were determined to leave for Calcutta. In the middle of September an event occurred that brought joy and encouragement into the Judsons' lives, for two young missionaries, James Colman and Edward M. Wheelock, arrived with their wives from America. The populace of Rangoon was as excited as Ann and Adoniram and crowded onto the shore to watch them unload their belongings.

Unfortunately the young men, both in their early twenties, were very frail. On their arrival in Rangoon their health was so bad that they were spitting blood. So ill was

Wheelock that he could hardly leave his bed. His wife Eliza, aged twenty, was most disappointed with conditions in the mission house, taking an instant dislike to Ann. She had arrived expecting to be treated as a heroine come from afar to convert the heathen. Instead she found a well-organized household already under the capable direction of another young woman not much older than herself.

This mission house had originally been built to house at the most two families, whereas with the arrival of the Wheelocks and Colmans it had to accommodate four, comprising eight grownups including the Houghs and three children (the two young Houghs and Emily). There were six rooms and a meeting place or chapel. Thinking to be kind, particularly on account of Wheelock's appalling state of health, the Judsons assigned him and his wife to the two coolest and driest rooms in the center of the house. For some reason these did not connect, something that Mrs. Wheelock made it her business to report in a letter to Mrs. Baldwin, wife of the Reverend Doctor Thomas Baldwin of the Second Church in Boston and the Mission Board's secretary.

At last, on November 1, 1818, the Hough family left for Calcutta, somewhat easing the accommodation problem if not Eliza Wheelock's discontent. She hated having to learn from Ann, who had already had six years' experience in the running of the communal mission house. She had expected to discover all kinds of hidden dangers and fantastic adventures in faraway Burma, but her daily tasks seemed to be little different from those expected of an ordinary New England housewife.

Meantime even if Adoniram was inwardly disappointed at the inadequacy through sickness of his new missionary colleagues, he did not show it. Instead, encouraged by Ann,

122

he plunged enthusiastically into a new project—the building of his own *zayat*.

A *zayat* was a small building where Buddhist lay preachers could give instruction. The Judsons' was the first Christian *zayat* ever built in Burma. It cost two hundred dollars and it was almost thirty feet long and twenty feet wide. The thatched bamboo porch in front had steps leading up to it. Inside, the walls were covered with whitewashed boards, while the windows were glassless openings.

On Sunday, April 4, 1819, they held their first service, for with Adoniram's return the mission's troubles seemingly disappeared. He had quickly rallied it together again and now, sitting on the porch of his new *zayat*, he invited the Burmese to enter.

"Ho! Everyone that thirsteth for knowledge," he shouted over and over. The result was a first congregation of fifteen grownups and a large number of curious children, the latter naked except for their colorful bracelets, necklaces and trinkets.

Actually the adults were as curious as the children, although they were much more interested in Adoniram's new suit, made by a Bengalese tailor, and Ann's laced ankle-boots, than the service. They made loud comments concerning both the clothes and the construction of the *zayat* so that, try as they would, the young American teachers had difficulty in keeping their congregation quiet for any length of time. Afterwards Adoniram decided that they had better attend a service in a Buddhist *zayat* and try to find the best way to hold the full attention of a Burmese congregation.

The first thing they did on entering was respectfully to remove their footwear. Then they seated themselves on mats that were provided, Adoniram on one side with the menfolk and Ann among the women on the other.

"There come some wild foreigners," announced a Burmese woman. Ann blushed scarlet.

"No, they are not wild; they are civilized," said a man who had watched Adoniram and Ann remove their footwear.

"It is the teacher," murmured somebody, recognizing Adoniram. "And his eminent wife," added another in a loud whisper.

In the center of the *zayat* the preacher was sitting on a low stand that rose about a foot from the ground. Immediately he spoke words of welcome, although his face fell when somebody informed him that the foreign visitors were themselves teachers of religion. Three times one of the worshippers asked for silence; then everybody with the exception of the Judsons took a flower and leaves, placing them between their fingers and then raising them to their heads. Throughout the service the congregation remained perfectly motionless with the flowers held in this position. The sermon lasted half an hour, at the end of which everybody prayed aloud. Then they filed quietly out.

The two Christian missionaries had to admit that the service was much more orderly than their own had been. The following Sunday Adoniram tried again in his own *zayat* and this time the congregation was better behaved. Every day he would sit on the porch looking out on Pagoda Road, inviting people in to talk. This was a particularly busy street for it led to the important Shwe-Dagon Pagoda. All along the way there were smaller pagodas, *zayats* and many homes. At all times thousands of tiny bells could be heard tinkling merrily in the wind.

The Burmese special day of worship came four times a month and was governed by the change of the moon. Then,

124

all day long, processions of faithful multitudes carrying lighted tapers and flowering blossoms walked along Pagoda Road to the great temple at the end. Thousands more crowded the busy thoroughfare for the annual religious festivals.

The *zayat* was now drawing more visitors every day, but none was more welcome than a poor man named Maung Nau. He came back several times while the two teachers hoped and prayed for his continued interest in their religion. "I begin to think that the Grace of God has reached his heart," Adoniram wrote at the time. He was right, for after six years of praying for a convert the Judsons watched with joy in their hearts as Maung Nau suddenly stood up before a congregation of thirty people and loudly confessed his belief in Jesus.

Thirty-five years old, employed by a timber merchant, Maung Nau had no family. He was a hard-working man. A few weeks after his first appearance at their *zayat* the young Burmese presented Adoniram with a letter that began,

I, Maung Nau, the constant recipient of your excellent favor, approach your feet. Whereas my lords three have come to the country of Burmah, not for the purpose of trade, but to preach the religion of Jesus Christ, the Son of the eternal God, I, having heard and understood, am, with a joyful mind, filled with love.

The first Burmese convert was duly baptized in a pond close to the Judsons' *zayat*. Adoniram reverently led him down into the water while Ann stood above—ironically, beneath an enormous statue of the Buddha—accompanied by a crowd of wondering men, women and children.

thirteen

King Bodawpaya died in his golden palace at Ava. The whole of Burma was seething with gossip, rumor and unrest, for the death of a monarch could result in civil war.

Adoniram wandered slowly through the silent, worried crowds down to the river bank. It was a beautiful clear morning; he had never seen the water look so inviting. Then he caught sight of the royal dispatch boat coming round the river bend and, fascinated, watched as it glided inshore.

The people began to whisper, politely making way for the sacred messengers, then following them to the high court where the city officials were waiting.

At last the sacred messengers proclaimed, "Listen ye: The immortal king, wearied, it would seem, with the fatigues of royalty, has gone up to amuse himself in the celestial regions. His grandson, the heir-apparent, is seated on the throne. The young monarch enjoins on all to remain quiet, and wait his imperial orders."

In fact, King Bodawpaya had been dead for two weeks but during that period things had been far from quiet in the golden city. As the first act of his reign the new King Bagyidaw had ordered his uncle the Prince of Toung Oo to be strangled, while other close relatives with near claims to the throne were sewn up in red sacks, as became royalty, and drowned. At least fourteen hundred noblemen and over ten thousand others were also put to death before King Bagyidaw felt his reign would be peaceful.

At the mission the Judsons decided to carry on with their work just as before. Ann, who was still teaching the women, rather enjoyed running her Burmese household. She was also learning Siamese, becoming proficient enough to translate her own little catechism, together with Adoniram's tract and St. Matthew's Gospel, into that language. Then for her own amusement she put a Siamese book into English. Its theme, she explains in her journal, was the incarnation of one of their deities when he existed in the form of a great elephant—a rather surprising choice for a Christian missionary's wife.

Little Emily was enjoying life in the mission, chattering happily away in Burmese. Like Ann, in mingling daily with the mission household she had picked up the language very quickly. Years later, as an old woman, she could still remember a Burmese hymn that Ann had taught her, and the memory of it brought tears to her eyes.

Other new families joined those already installed at the mission. Actually they were squatters, who had taken the liberty of building crude bamboo shelters in the compound and started housekeeping. Among them was a young woman Mah Baik, her husband, and brother Maung Thalah. The latter was a quiet, gentle man who quickly responded to Adoniram's teaching. Ann decided to see if she could also interest his sister, but Mah Baik presented a problem: her favorite occupation was quarreling. It was a pleasure she found hard to resist and at the least provocation she went into a terrible rage, which she thoroughly enjoyed.

Ann tried hard to explain that Christians *should not quarrel* and to join them Mah Baik would have to control her tempestuous emotions. With a long face she admitted Ann might be right but it was simply asking too much to expect her to keep her temper.

This was one occasion where even the Hasseltine charm failed, although Ann's pride was somewhat placated to see Adoniram's success at converting Mah Baik's gentle-tempered brother. Maung Thalah, together with Maung Byaay, a man of fifty who had been taught to read and write in the Christian *zayat*, were to have the distinction of being the second and third Burmese to be baptized. As before, the ceremony took place in the pool beneath the Buddha, only this time at dusk. During the short time the new King had reigned the missionaries had been disturbed by several incidents.

The converts, recognizing the need for such a private ceremony, had themselves searched the gospels to see if John the Baptist had baptized at any special hour. To their intense satisfaction they discovered he had not; so in petitioning Adoniram they said, "We, therefore, venture to beg of the two teachers, that they will grant, that on the 6th day of the wane of the Tanzoungmong moon, at 6 o'clock at night, we may this once receive baptism at their hands."

Adoniram was not happy about the need for secrecy,

but on talking it over with Ann he agreed that the early Christians had provided many precedents for such discretion.

As was to be expected, the Buddhist priests and teachers in Rangoon were not pleased at the building of the *zayat* or the new interest in the Christian religion. One man, called the Mangen Teacher, was particularly incensed when he heard that a wealthy and intellectual Burmese had actually visited the Judsons to inquire after the new religion. It was time, he thought, to drop a timely word in the viceroy's hearing. The Mangen Teacher was in turn instructed to find out more, whereupon hearing this, Maung Shway-gnong, the wealthy Burmese, decided Christianity was altogether too dangerous a religion for him.

Pleased with this minor success, the Mangen Teacher set out early one morning to intercept the Judsons as they rode on horseback to a mineral pond for their daily bath. He had taken care to discover their route, which was on the way to the Shwe-Dagon Pagoda. Pouncing on the unsuspecting missionaries, he screamed in a loud voice that if they rode again on any road leading to the most important of all the pagodas he would order them both to be beaten.

Very upset, the couple returned to the mission to find that the viceroy had indeed issued a mandate declaring that no person "wearing a hat, shoes, or umbrella, or mounted on a horse, shall approach within the sacred ground belonging to the great pagoda." The missionaries knew the order was directed at them because they were the only residents wearing hats and shoes to ride horses.

Adoniram at once decided that if the Christian mission were to carry on unmolested, permission must be obtained from the highest authority in the land, the new King Bagyidaw himself. If he allowed the missionaries to teach, nobody would dare interfere. Adoniram in person would lay a petition before the Golden Feet.

They had one special friend at the royal court, Mya-daymen, the spear-stalking former viceroy of Rangoon whose wife was Ann's dear friend. He had been promoted to the exalted rank of Wungyi or prime minister, enjoying a position next in importance to the King himself. Because of her great friendship with the new Wungyi's wife Ann wished to accompany Adoniram to Ava, but he decided it was not wise. Never before had a Christian missionary made a personal petition to a Burmese king asking for permission to teach his subjects a new religion. It was almost an impertinence, and to take his wife when no foreign woman had ever set foot in Ava might well be disastrous.

Ann did not altogether agree. Once before, at Mya-daymen's own court when they first came to Rangoon, she had been successful with officialdom when her husband had failed, for the simple reason that she was a foreign woman.

However she had problems of her own to contend with, for Eliza Wheelock, still obsessed with her own selfish disappointment at not finding herself a heroine, failed (or refused) to recognize how ill her poor young husband was. Daily he grew more emaciated and when the other members of the mission, particularly the Judsons, tactfully warned her she became even more enraged and insulted. Although Eliza herself had written down the fact that "a European, favored with health and a good appetite could, I think, live almost entirely upon the productions of the country" she could not have had her health-lacking husband in mind. In spite of Ann's "experimenting" and so adding a few new dishes to the monotonous daily diet, such as a concoction of pounded rice, plantains and vegetables, the staple dish was

131

the same curried fowl, rice and vegetables that the Judsons had found when they first arrived in 1813 at Rangoon.

Adoniram asked Ann to speak to Eliza as one woman to another concerning Wheelock's condition, for it was now apparent to everybody but her that he was not long for this world. When Ann did so Eliza became even more incensed, immediately demanding that Ann should provide the kind of foods and comforts that were simply unobtainable in Burma.

Whatever Christian principles Eliza had ever possessed—and she must have had some to have married a missionary—they were sadly lacking in the events that followed. Nothing that either the Judsons or Colmans did to ease her husband's sufferings (the Houghs having finally returned to Calcutta) pleased her. *They were, she decided, trying to shut her out.* When Ann "invented" custards and delicacies to please the invalid's cravings, Eliza became more vindictive than ever.

Although Wheelock particularly enjoyed Ann's visits with her lively talk of the progress made in the mission—a pleasing subject to a young man who had first made up his mind at the age of eighteen to make a missionary's life his career—even these were finally forbidden by the jealous Mrs. Wheelock. She became suspicious of everybody connected with the mission, including the very Burmese her husband had purposely come to "save." She decided that the Judsons in particular were trying to separate her husband from her, continually voicing her suspicions to him. She tried hard to persuade him that his very life depended upon their "escaping" to Bengal, conveniently forgetting that it was the worst possible time of year for sea travel and that Wheelock was a very bad sailor, suffering all the time from bouts of seasickness. Wheelock, to his credit, took little

132

notice of her mistaken notions until he became at last too weak and delirious to resist them. Finally Eliza insisted on their leaving although her husband seemed on the point of dying. It was a sad way for missionaries to part; Eliza was unforgiving to the end.

Thirteen days out of Rangoon Wheelock, in a state of pain-crazed madness, escaped from his cabin, ran on deck and jumped overboard. He was never seen again.

Eliza lost little time in remarrying, this time to "a Mr. Jones of Calcutta." She made it her business to write many letters to friends in America telling complete fabrications of the Judsons' ill treatment of the sick Wheelock. When Ann eventually heard of this she was deeply hurt, and made it her immediate business to write Wheelock's aged parents, telling them that she did not want them to think that she was "so destitute of the feelings of humanity as to have denied their son anything which could have rendered him comfortable." In plain words she declared that Eliza Wheelock had been the "root of bitterness" adding, "we are endeavouring to cultivate a forgiving spirit, and I trust we have in some measure obtained it."

Young Colman's health improved, however, and by the time Adoniram was ready to leave for Ava he seemed quite recovered. The two men had designed themselves surplice-like white robes to wear at the golden court for they did not think their dark clerical suits sufficiently impressive for a royal court. As a gift they had decided to take the King a handsome Bible written in English. It comprised six large volumes which they had covered with expensive gold leaf and enclosed in a rich cover.

A week passed before Adoniram found a river boat willing to take them to Ava. It was forty feet long with a great prow carved like a dragon's head. A high seat at the stern was provided for the steersman, complete with an elaborate umbrella placed there as a symbol of his importance.

Orders were given for a bamboo deck to be laid and a small cabin built, large enough for the missionaries to use for sleeping purposes. Armed with a permit granted by the Rangoon viceroy, the dragon-boat with its passengers and gifts at last set sail for the Golden City. Ann, sadly disappointed, watched it go. Next day, December 22, 1819, would be her thirtieth birthday.

The crew comprised the all-important steersman and ten oarsmen. There were in addition two cooks, one for the missionaries and another, Maung Nau, for the rest. Also on board were a "headsman" acting as official government representative, an Englishman described as having been "unfortunate all his life and wishing to try the service of his Burmese majesty," and a Hindu washerman. An armament of guns and blunderbusses had been provided, with the "unfortunate Englishman" in charge, for the river was infested by pirates. At various villages along the way they heard how these pirates, known as Dacoits, attacked boats and plundered shipping.

At the head of the delta the Rangoon River joined the mighty Irrawaddy. The paddy fields gave way to lush tropical forests filled with bananas, tamarinds and mangoes. They passed great rafts loaded with teak, rickety rice ships and dozens of lesser craft, some so fragile-looking it seemed miraculous that their crew could control them. Where the forest had been cleared, small fishing villages clustered about the river banks. Adoniram would never forget the smell of

134

fresh *ngapi* made of spiced, rotting fish which was used like salt or pepper.

The villages were dwarfed by the imposing ruins of past civilizations. Mighty temples and palaces, left to decay and crumble on the death of the king who had built them, rose out of the forests. In the background were yellow-flecked mountains and deep green valleys. Monkeys screamed and chattered among the twisting vines that over-hung the river. Tree-rats scrambled between the clumps of ripening green bananas.

Spread out on a great plain was the ancient city of Pagan with five thousand temples. Adoniram had read that in Pagan Buddhism had been chosen as the official Burmese religion some eight centuries before. Here too the huge statue in rock-hewn blocks portraying the Thandawgya Buddha had been built in 1284. The frescoed ceilings and walls of the Ananda Monastery were spoken of as one of Burma's many wonders.

In the Shwegu Temple was a prayer written by King Alaungsithu (1112-1167). In Pali verse, it began,

By this my gift, whatever boon I seek
It is the best of boons to profit all.

Adoniram, who was growing to respect the Burmese culture, could not fail to be moved by its simplicity or meaning. He wondered at the implacable urge that drove men to erect sixteen square miles of such monuments when instead they might have built rich palaces for themselves.

As they neared Ava, warnings of river pirates became even more frequent. At nightfall about four days before they hoped to reach the golden city, and after a month on the river, the worst happened. They had anchored in a sheltered spot when, without warning, a boatload of the most desperate-looking group of men Adoniram had ever seen descended shouting upon them. However, the head-man had the presence of mind to fire a musket over the attackers' craft, which seemed to make them change their minds. Shouting at the dragon boat to cease firing, the pirates disappeared into the blackness.

Adoniram and Colman were badly shaken by the un-pleasant incident and it was with much relief that they landed four miles below Ava on January 25, 1820. There were actually two Avas, one of which had been built during a former dynasty. The new city was often called Amarapura and here the Golden Presence, King Bagyidaw, held his court. The Dragon boat dropped anchor at Sagaing, a hamlet famed for its many pagodas. Once the seat of the old Kings of Burma, it has today regained much of its former importance under the name of Mandalay, second largest city in the country.

Adoniram's first task was to get in touch with Mya-day-men. The new Wungyi was now so important he had been elevated to the rank of Hlutdau, or member of the council of state comprising only four chief officials. The King also had a privy council of four men known as Atwinwuns. No-body seemed to be able to decide who were more important, the Hlutdaus or the Atwinwuns.

Mya-day-men's house lay four miles away in the walled city of Amarapura. The missionaries set out on foot, followed by Maung Nau, their convert, together with several crew members carrying gifts of cloth.

Close to the city lived two men who merited courtesy calls. Now Burmese subjects but English by birth, they had left India years before for reasons best known to themselves. One of them, Rodgers, had once been fourth mate on a ship. In 1782 he had attacked the first mate with a loaded cane commonly called a "Penang lawyer," which necessitated his leaving the East India Company territory. He was now married to a Burmese woman of Portuguese descent, who had borne him a child. Rodgers still spoke with a heavy Yorkshire brogue, and in spite of his Burmese clothing looked very conspicuous with his blue eyes and carefully thinned beard. For years he had been maneuvering for the tax collector's appointment in Rangoon, his rival for favor being a Spaniard named Lanciego. Adoniram expected little help from Rodgers who at that time was unpopular at the golden court. In any case he would hardly want to intercede on behalf of a cause so delicate as the Christian mission.

Gibson, the other Englishman, had in the past been friendly toward the Judsons.

Amarapura itself was an imposing city enclosed by a high wall, on every corner of which stood a solid-looking brick pagoda. Within the square mile enclosed by this wall stood the palace, a great rambling affair surrounded by government buildings and the homes of the nobles. Everywhere Adoniram and Colman looked, their eyes were blinded by dazzling roof tops that were actually covered with gold. The dusty streets were unpaved; the servants lived in huts whose meagre appearance did not match the grandeur of the palace within whose shadow they stood.

At the gate Adoniram courteously inquired the way to Mya-day-men's house and was told that it stood beyond the palace. The once feared Mya-day-men greeted his friend with real feeling, and as for his wife, she could hardly contain her emotion as she inquired after "Mrs. Yoodthan," as she called Ann. Of course they were anxious to know the reason for Adoniram's sudden visit to the capital, but he

137

thought it wise to be evasive. They were satisfied when he
told them that Colman and he had made the journey because
they wished to see with their own eyes the Golden Presence
in the Golden City of Ava. Immediately Mya-day-men
agreed to help them to obtain their greatly desired audience.
It came much sooner than they anticipated, which em-
phasized Mya-day-men's new importance as Wungyi. The
same evening they learned the King would see them next
day.

fourteen

That night the two young men hardly slept at all. After more than six years in Burma, Adoniram was at last to meet the one man who could help or destroy the mission he had labored so long to build. When morning came they hurriedly washed in the river before putting on their spotless white robes in readiness for the royal audience.

Maung Yo, an official well thought of by Mya-day-men, arrived to conduct them back to their friend's home. Members of the crew acted as gift-bearers, carrying the Bible which had been so expensively covered with gold leaf.

Mya-day-men again greeted the missionaries warmly. He told them that on hearing of their arrival in Amarapura the Golden Presence had declared, "Let them be introduced."

Then the procession through the hot, dusty streets began, Maung Yo leading the way surrounded by a host of chattering attendants. At the palace gate there was a long delay while permits were examined. Finally a present was left, footwear was removed, and the procession moved into the enormous audience hall of Maung Zah the Atwinwun. It was so large, with such towering columns, that even Adoniram's natural exuberance seemed subdued. Hundreds of important dignitaries, retainers and minor officials were in evidence, and Maung Zah sat on a low dais-like throne. The dignitaries were carefully seated according to rank, with governors in front. Adoniram and Colman were honored by being made to sit in front of everybody else.

Maung Zah was not unfriendly. Cordially he inquired the purpose of their visit to which Adoniram replied that they were "propagators of religion," adding that they wished to give the King a petition, together with their sacred books. Maung Zah expressed a wish to examine the petition, which was then handed to him. He read for a little while and asked a few questions, which Adoniram answered tactfully. Suddenly an official arrived with the message "The Golden Foot is about to advance." Instantly all was confusion, the crowd, with the exception of a chosen few, seeming to melt into the floor. As for Maung Zah, he jumped to his feet, while several attendants stepped quickly forward with his robes of state. He did manage to say that if the teachers were to meet the King it would have to be now.

Fascinated, the missionaries watched closely as the good-looking Atwinwun arranged his golden chain of office known as a *tsalway*. Made up of twelve beautifully adorned strands, it was worn in such a way that it crossed on his breast. A *tsalway* was the highest insignia given to any

Burmese subject; ordinarily only a prince of the royal blood might wear it.

So absorbed was Maung Zah with his dressing that he temporarily forgot the two missionaries. A courtier made it his business to inform them that this was the anniversary of the Burmese victory over the Cassays. The Golden Feet were advancing so that the Golden Eyes might see a special military display honoring the great event. They had chosen a most unfortunate day to present a petition, particularly one asking indulgence for a foreign religion. In eager anticipation of an exciting military display the Golden Presence would hardly feel happy at being delayed.

"How can you propagate religion in this empire?" interrupted Maung Zah who at last was through with his titivating. Then "Come along," he said with an air of impatience, hurrying them from the room.

Somewhat disillusioned, they followed him through a maze of passages that terminated in a brilliant audience hall, each section of which was covered with gold, including the pillars surrounding the umbrellalike dome. Adoniram glanced self-consciously at their golden Bible, a mere raindrop surrounded by an ocean of gold. But there was little time for misgivings, for all around him men were throwing themselves onto their faces. Maung Yo managed to whisper that the Golden Feet had arrived. With folded hands the missionaries knelt, feeling both eager and afraid at the awesome prospect of seeing the Burmese king.

The Golden Presence had marched unattended into the room. He was a little man, just over five feet tall and very bowlegged. As he strode in with "the proud gait and majesty of an Eastern monarch," he was judged by Adoniram to be about twenty-eight years old. His face was not unpleasant but was spoiled somewhat by a curious slanted forehead inherited from the emperor Alompra. The King's *engyee* or jacket was made of white muslin, while his *patso* was of the scarlet only royalty might wear. His knotted, turbanlike headdress enclosed his long black hair. Adoniram was more impressed by the elaborate sword with its golden sheath than by his costume.

The Golden Presence could not fail to notice the Americans, even in so large a reception hall, for they were the only men in the room who were not prostrated before him.

"Who are these?" he demanded.

Adoniram did not give anyone the satisfaction of answering for him. In excellent Burmese he replied, "The teachers, Great King."

The Golden Presence was noticeably shaken. "What, you speak Burmese? The priests that I heard of last night? When did you arrive?"

Adoniram swallowed hard before replying. He was gaining confidence. "Yesterday, Your Majesty."

King Bagyidaw was, if nothing else, agreeably surprised to hear his own language spoken by a foreign teacher. He was also impressed by Adoniram's soft, courteous voice and good manners. The Golden Eyes strayed toward Colman, who wisely and with some relief left all the talking to his more experienced colleague. Then the Golden Presence arranged himself on a dais, all the time keeping his hand on his sword hilt, while he carefully studied each missionary in turn. Still lying flat on their faces, his own subjects gingerly tried to peek at what, to say the least, was a most unusual spectacle.

Then the King asked in an interested voice, "Are you teachers of religion?"

"Yes," Adoniram replied.

"Are you married? Are you like the Portuguese priests?

142

Why do you dress as you do? On hearing the last question
Adoniram looked somewhat uncomfortably at his new
surplicelike robe. The King asked a few other minor questions and then was silent. Maung Zah, who all this time
had been lying flat on the floor awaiting his cue, slowly
lifted his face and proceeded to read the all-important
petition:

The American teachers present themselves to receive
the favor of the excellent king, the sovereign of land and
sea.

Hearing that, on account of the greatness of the royal
power, the royal country was in a quiet and prosperous
state, we arrived at the town of Rangoon, within the royal
dominions, and having obtained leave from the governor
of that town, to come up and behold the Golden Face,
we have ascended, and reached the bottom of the Golden
Feet.

In the great country of America we sustain the character
of teachers and explainers of the contents of the sacred
Scriptures of our religion. And since it is contained in
those Scriptures, that, if we pass to other countries, and
preach and propagate religion, great good will result, and
both those who teach and those who receive the religion
will be freed from future punishment, and enjoy, without
decay or death, the eternal felicity of heaven—that royal
permission be given, that we, taking refuge in the royal
power, may preach our religion in these dominions, and
that those who are pleased with our preaching, and wish
to listen to and be guided by it, whether foreigners or
Burmans, may be exempt from Government molestation,
they present themselves to receive the favor of the excellent king, the sovereign of land and sea.

The King held out his hand for the petition so that
Maung Zah was obliged to crawl forward in order to
present it. Then the Golden Eyes carefully read it through,

143

while Adoniram handed Maung Zah a copy of his tract specially abridged for the occasion. As the Golden Eyes turned to the tract Adoniram silently prayed, "Oh have mercy on Burma! Have mercy on her king!"

Bagyidaw began to read, "There is one Being who exists eternally; who is exempt from sickness, old age, and death; who is, and was, and will be, without beginning and without end. Besides this, the true God, there is no other God——"

The Golden Eyes flashed with anger; with contempt the Golden Hands threw the offending tract on the floor. Maung Yo coaxingly opened a gold-covered volume of the Bible to show the King but there was no response.

Maung Zah then spoke for the Golden Lips.

"Why do you ask for such permission? Have not the Portuguese, the English, the Moslems, and people of all other religions, full liberty to practice and worship according to their own customs? In regard to the objects of your petition, His Majesty gives no order. In regard to your sacred books, His Majesty has no use for them. Take them away."

Then the Golden Feet walked off in the direction of the military display, leaving a dejected Adoniram Judson behind them.

fifteen

E ven the thought of further encounters with river pirates failed to trouble Adoniram as the boat with the dragon's head sailed rapidly downstream on the homeward journey to Rangoon. He was too disappointed and upset. "I could moralize half an hour on the apt resemblance, the beautiful congruity, between the desolate state of our feelings and the sandy barren surface of this miserable beach," he wrote just before leaving the Golden City. "But 'tis idle all. Let the beach and our sorrow go together. Something better will turn up tomorrow."

They had even found it difficult to get a passport out of Amarapura. Five days had been wasted in wrangling arguments. In the end it took a bribe to get one. Following the King's rebuttal of their petition, Gibson the friendly Englishman had tried to help them. He even took them to the Atwinwun Maung Zah's home, but he only received them with coldness and hostility. To have presented the King with such a petition asking for religious tolerance was an unpardonable offence. Maung Zah considered the teachers fortunate to have left the palace unpunished.

Gibson cleverly suggested that if the American missionaries could once obtain the King's favor other foreigners would surely visit Burma. From such friendship increased trade would result. This last argument seemed to impress Maung Zah, but nevertheless next day he sent Gibson a message saying, "Tell them that there is not the least possibility of obtaining the object stated in this paper should they wait ever so long." But he had read "this paper" (Adoniram's tract) and even conceded "The doctrine and commands are very good—but it will be a long time before Burmans can be convinced there is a God and Saviour."

Bravely Gibson had even mentioned the teachers once more to the King. "What," he cried with a laugh, "they have come presuming to convert us to their religion! Let them leave our capital. We have no desire to receive their instruction. Perhaps they may find some of their countrymen in Rangoon who may be willing to listen to them."

Gibson strongly advised Adoniram to get a royal order of protection. "Otherwise," he said, "as it will be notorious that you have solicited royal patronage and been refused, you will lie at the mercy of every ill-disposed person." With unpleasant memories of the time Ann and he were set upon by the jealous Mangen Teacher while riding horseback to their bathing place, Adoniram appreciated the wisdom of obtaining such a royal order. Unfortunately

146

it would doubtless cost more money than the missionaries could afford.

Rodgers, the Yorkshireman with the goatlike beard, told Adoniram that a Christian mission would be futile, but Adoniram well knew that any foreigner, whether missionary or not, would be unwelcome to this power-seeking man. The Yorkshire man did, however, give them some interesting information concerning the Chief Queen under whose complete domination the young monarch lived. The daughter of a jailer belonging to the lowest class in the land and older than her husband, she had managed to advance from her lowly position of being one among many concubines to the regal status of first wife. She was a religious fanatic and her power was feared throughout the court. Some Burmese decided she must be a witch; otherwise how could the daughter of a mere jailer have managed to put even the King under her evil influence? On the day following the missionaries' visit the King had created a hundred new priests, some of them members of the most noble families in the land. He had feasted, at a special palace banquet, all Buddhist priests living in the vicinity of the Golden City.

Then there was the Atwinwun or privy councilor who hated the Chistian religion so much that he had personally accused his own uncle, a Roman Catholic convert, and seen him put to the torture many years before. The uncle, who refused to recant, was only released because somebody told the king of that time that the prisoner was insane. Portuguese priests had then taken him secretly to Bengal where later he died.

The Golden Presence was naturally going to be prejudiced against the teaching of a foreign religion with such advisers as this particular Atwinwun and the hostile Queen.

147

When the dragon boat reached Prone, a hundred miles above Rangoon, Adoniram was greeted by the eminent middle-aged scholar Maung Shway-gnong. An old acquaintance of this scholar, Adoniram had once said, "He is the most powerful reasoner I have yet met with in this country except my old teacher Oo Oungmen, and he is not at all inferior to him." But Maung Shway-gnong was to prove a bitter disappointment to both Adoniram and Ann, who also enjoyed talking with him, for, on the point of becoming a Christian, Maung Shway-gnong had suddenly lost all interest. The Mangen Teacher had made it his business to inform the viceroy in Rangoon of his fellow scholar's apparent curiosity in the "foreign religion" and Maung Shway-gnong, fearing reprisals, had faded as gracefully as he could from Adoniram's life. The missionary, who had been hurt and disgusted, now found himself once more in the company of the man he had so much respected. Maung Shway-gnong was visiting a sick friend in Prone.

Feeling rather sorry for himself, Adoniram told the Burmese scholar the story of his unsuccessful trip to the Golden Feet. His former friend took the news so calmly that the missionary became quite upset.

"It is not for you that we are concerned," complained Adoniram, "but for those who have become disciples of Christ. When they are accused and persecuted, they cannot worship at the pagodas and recant before the Mangen Teacher as you have done."

The scholar, shifting his feet uneasily, started to speak but Adoniram was not in the mood for excuses.

"Say nothing," he shouted. "One thing you know to be true—that when formerly accused, if you had not in some way or other satisfied the Mangen Teacher, your life would not now be remaining in your body."

148

A long pause followed; then the scholar earnestly declared himself to be a new man. "If I must die, I shall die in a good cause," he promised. "I know it is the cause of truth. I believe in the eternal God, in His Son Jesus Christ, in the atonement which Christ has made, and in the writings of the apostles, as the true and only word of God."

Adoniram then boarded the dragon boat and sat down, beckoning Maung Shway-gnong to do the same. With the waves gently rocking them, Maung Shway-gnong continued: "Perhaps you may not remember that during one of my last visits you told me that I was trusting in my own understanding rather than the divine word. From that time I have seen my error, and endeavored to renounce it. You explained to me also the evil of worshiping at pagodas, though I told you that my heart did not partake in the worship. Since you left Rangoon I have not lifted my folded hands before a pagoda. It is true, I sometimes follow the crowd on days of worship in order to avoid persecution, but I walk up one side of the pagoda and walk down the other. Now you say that I am not a disciple. What lack I yet?"

Adoniram cleared his throat. He knew the scholar had spoken honestly, and wished to answer him in like vein. At last he said, "You may be a disciple of Christ in heart, but you are not a full disciple. You have not faith and resolution enough to keep all the commands of Christ, particularly that which requires you to be baptized, though in the face of persecution and death. Consider the words of Jesus just before He returned to heaven: '*He that believeth and is baptized shall be saved.*'"

Maung Shway-gnong was silent. Then Adoniram told him that the missionaries might be forced to leave Rangoon, for when they heard how the King had received the teacher, the Burmese would be too frightened to listen to the Christian lessons.

"Say not so," begged the scholar. "There are some who will investigate, notwithstanding; and rather than have you leave Rangoon, I will myself go to the Mangen Teacher and have a public dispute. I know I can silence him."

At this even Adoniram had to smile. "Yes, you may have a tongue to silence *him*—but he has a pair of fetters and an iron maul to silence you!"

Long after the scholar had gone Adoniram pondered over their strange reunion. Was God giving him a sign? Here in the very face of defeat he had met quite by chance a man who had once renounced Christianity, yet now was offering to stand up publicly and defend it!

February 18, 1820. Rangoon—home—and best of all, Ann. She was there waiting when the dragon boat glided silently to the shore. It seemed to Adoniram she was always waiting when he needed her most. Love and pride welled up in his heart as he caught the first glimpse of his wife holding an umbrella to shelter her face from the sun. "She is my right hand," he thought. "God forbid she may ever be taken from me."

As soon as possible Adoniram met with Maung Nau, Maung Thahlah and Maung Byaay, his faithful first converts, to tell them personally of the failure of his journey to Ava. He reminded them that without the King's royal protection the Burmese Christians could expect nothing but persecution, torture or death. He felt that it might even be best for the missionaries themselves to leave Burma rather than increase the danger to their converts. Adoniram secretly believed Maung Thahlah and Maung Byaay might even renounce Christianity in the face of such overwhelming odds. Of Maung Nau he was sure, for on the journey back from Ava he had told Adoniram that he was ready to follow the missionaries wherever they might go, being only afraid that his inability to speak another language might prove a hindrance to his supporting himself, as he did not wish to become a liability.

Adoniram was wrong, for the more he spoke of dangers to be expected the greater became the enthusiasm of the three converts.

"Where are the teachers going?" The all-important question was asked by each convert in turn. Adoniram replied that he was considering Chittagong where there were already Baptist converts. Recently their missionary, de Bruyn, had been murdered. The three converts listened carefully. For Maung Thahlah the decision would be an easy one. "I go where preaching is to be done," he declared emphatically.

For Maung Byaay it was not so easy. Burmese women were forbidden to travel beyond the boundaries of their own land and he had both wife and children. "If I must be left here alone, I shall remain performing the duties of Jesus Christ's religion," he said in a quiet voice. "No other shall I think of."

So the matter of leaving Burma was tentatively settled. With sad hearts Adoniram and Colman set about finding a ship bound for Chittagong. A few days later Adoniram was surprised to receive a visit from Maung Byaay, accompanied by Maung Myat-yah, his brother-in-law, who had often attended services in the Judsons' *zayat*, and whose home was a hut in the mission compound. After formally greeting Adoniram, Maung Byaay announced, "I

151

have come to petition that you will not leave Rangoon at present."

Adoniram felt a lump thicken in his throat, for the man's simple approach touched him deeply. "I think it is useless to remain under the present circumstances," he answered in a broken voice. "We cannot open the *zayat*. We cannot have public worship. No Burmese will dare to examine this religion; and if none examine, none will embrace it."

"Teacher, my mind is distressed. I can neither eat nor sleep since I find you are going away," pleaded Maung Byaay. "I have talked with those who live near us, and I find some who are even now examining the new religion. Brother Myat-yah is one, and he unites with me in my petition. Therefore do stay with us a few months. Stay until there are eight or ten disciples. Then appoint one to be the teacher of the rest. I shall not be concerned about the event. Though you leave the country, the religion will spread of itself. The King himself cannot stop it. But if you go now, and take the two disciples that can follow, I shall be left alone. I cannot baptize those who may wish to embrace this religion. What can I do?"

This was too much for Adoniram. He felt that he must talk the matter over at once with Colman and Ann. Then the ever-faithful Maung Nau arrived. He was positive that in spite even of the King's opposition nothing could now stem the tide of converts.

Adoniram looked inquiringly at his wife, uncertain for the moment what to do while she steadfastly returned his gaze, as if to say, "You know what we must do." Secretly he felt ashamed even to have doubted the sincerity of two of their converts in the face of possible persecution. He returned to the unhappy men sitting on the verandah.

"We live only for the promotion of the cause of Christ

152

among the Burmese," he informed them. "If there is any prospect of success in Rangoon we have no desire to go to another place. Therefore we will reconsider the matter."

In the days that followed the three converts did their best to rally interest for the Christian cause. Little groups of interested people drifted up the steps leading to the mission house.

One evening Maung Thahlah told Adoniram, "Teacher, your intention of going away has filled us all with trouble. Is it good to forsake us thus? Notwithstanding present difficulties and dangers, it is to be remembered that this work is not yours or ours, but the work of God. If He give light, the religion will spread. Nothing can impede it."

Then Maung Byaay, raising his arm to be heard, took up the argument. "Let us all make an effort," he entreated. "As for me, I will pray. If we can get a little church of ten members, with one who is capable of administering the ordinances, then if you feel the necessity of going to another place to preach, go, and we will stay here and perform the duties of religion, in a still secret way, agreeably to the sacred writings. It is my opinion that there will be one raised up among us who is more learned than any of us, and who will be qualified to be our teacher. Though government difficulties are before us, hell is also before us, and those who are really afraid of hell cannot help embracing Christ."

"Yes," Maung Thahlah added, "Christ has taught us not to fear those who can kill the body only, but to fear him who can destroy both soul and body in hell."

There was silence while Adoniram pondered the words of his friends. A tiny green lizard ran up the wall, his back streaked yellow by the soft oil light. Ann appeared with tiny cups of green tea for their guests. Adoniram

153

glanced at her tired, drawn face. He knew she had not been sleeping well lately; at times a pain in her side was intense.

Late into the night the Judsons and Colmans discussed their joint problem. It was decided that the Colmans should be the ones to go to Chittagong; then if the Rangoon mission was forced into closing at least its work would not have been entirely in vain. The Judsons, with as many Burmese converts as possible, would then join them.

The decision pleased Ann, for she knew Adoniram too well. Often in the past she had heard him cry out in his sleep, "I long to reach the Golden Shore."

Burma was his golden shore; would he ever be happy elsewhere? Or, for that reason, would she?

sixteen

Regretfully the Judsons watched on March 17, 1820, as the Colmans sailed away. Mrs. Colman had been a particularly pleasant young woman, always useful and ready to learn. She had been a great help with the housekeeping and Ann hated to see her go, but it had to be.

No more did they dare hold services in their *zayat* on Pagoda Road for fear of reprisals. Instead they turned the room vacated by the Colmans into their "new *zayat*." Here quiet evening services could be held with comparative safety. Maung Nau was especially helpful. He appeared to them as a rock of strength in their present trouble so that often they affectionately called him "Peter" after that other Peter in the New Testament.

Maung Shway-gnong was still a problem. Although two of his wealthy friends applied for baptism, he continued to hold back, all the time asking questions. He argued that he could not see why one should worship on a special day of the week. Surely the other days were just as good as Sunday? He must read his Bible and pray for enlightenment. Adoniram was fast coming to the conclusion that the real reason for Maung Shway-gnong's reluctance to be baptized was not for lack of belief in Jesus Christ but simply because such a baptism would mean certain execution for so prominent a man.

In time even Adoniram began to feel sorry for his friend, recording, "My heart was wrung with pity. . . The thought of the iron maul, and a secret suspicion that if I was in his circumstances, I should perhaps have no more courage, restrained my tongue."

Ann was also fighting her own little battle to save the soul of Mah Men-lay, a Burmese woman of whom she had become particularly fond. She was having more success than with Mah Baik, the prospective convert who could not give up the pleasure of losing her temper!

The pretty Mah Men-lay, her sleek black hair carefully oiled and combed straight back from the temples, a fresh red flower worked into the coil on top of her head, would generally arrive in the company of a few other women to have tea and discuss the religion of Jesus with "Mrs. Yood-than." At all times she showed real interest but always Ann sensed the timid, quiet-spoken woman's fear of what would happen to her family should she embrace Christianity. Even so, Mah Men-lay's very fear seemed only to increase her urgent desire to add to her knowledge of the new teaching.

One afternoon Mah Men-lay startled Ann by saying, "I

am surprised to find this religion has such an effect on my mind as to make me love the disciples of Christ more than my dearest natural relatives."

As Ann well knew, this admission was no small thing to make, for most of Mah Men-lay's countrymen and women loved to have as many relatives as possible even if they were only cousins or in-laws. Their word for "relative" had the same root as that meaning "friend" and for the ten beings who merited their greatest love. This list began of course with the Buddha and the *arhats*—those who had reached the state of Nirvana—and included, with the parents, benefactors outside the family who could give one either material gifts or counsel and example in moral living.

Adoniram was secretly delighted at Ann's success with Mah Men-lay. He could not help hoping that his wife would be responsible for converting the first Burmese woman to Christianity. With much satisfaction he noted how Mah Men-lay continued to bring her friends in for tea and discussion. He was pleased to learn that one of these in the old royal city of Pegu had come across his tract. That had been six weeks before; yet after reading it she could not rest until she had made the long river journey to Rangoon for the purpose of learning more of the new religion. He wondered where next one of his writings would turn up.

Pleased as he was with his wife's fortitude in their present adversity, Adoniram found himself worrying about her. He would have liked to attribute the dark rings around her eyes and the yellowish pallor of her skin to overwork coupled with the intense heat, but in his heart he knew this was not the reason. Little by little life seemed to be slipping away from her. It appeared to his inexperienced

157

eyes that she was suffering from a form of liver ailment, but without proper medical advice he could not be sure. Ann hopefully tried two long and sickening home treatments of 'salivation'* but they only seemed to leave her feeling worse than when she began.

By June she was so ill that it seemed certain that if she did not see a doctor immediately there would be another grave beside little Roger's. It was even doubtful if she could make on her own the long sea voyage to Bengal where medical attention might be obtained. Emily Van Someren was not yet old or capable enough to be saddled with the responsibility of a sick woman aboard ship. There was nothing to do but accompany Ann. With the help of the Spaniard, Lanciego, who was still fighting the Yorkshire-born Rodgers over the lucrative tax collector's post in Rangoon, Adoniram managed to obtain passports for Ann, Emily and himself. Lanciego even promised to keep under his personal protection those people remaining in the mission compound while the Judsons were away.

There was a ship in the river waiting to leave but until it was ready Ann and Adoniram remained at their quarters in the mission. During this time the scholar Maung Shway-gnong called on them. Adoniram did not feel as cordial as usual because the wavering convert had remained away for some little time. However, the scholar explained he had been sick with a fever. As the visit wore on more of his friends arrived. Suddenly Maung Shway-gnong stood up and declared in a firm voice, "My lord teacher, there are now several of us who have long considered this religion. I hope that we are all believers in Jesus Christ."

* Salivation: a continuous unnatural flow of saliva, especially with soreness in the mouth and gums. To produce an abnormal amount of saliva Ann took mercury pills.

158

If Adoniram swallowed with surprise, so did Ann, who because of her sickness was resting behind the thin bamboo walls in an adjoining room. Had she really heard aright? If so, she could hardly believe her own ears. Surely it could not have been their own Doubting Thomas speaking? Then she caught Adoniram's reply.

"I am afraid to say that. However, it is easy to determine; and let me begin with you, teacher. I have heretofore thought that you fully believed in the eternal God; but I have some doubt whether you fully believed in the Son of God and the atonement which He has made."

The dignified face of the aging scholar looked appealingly at Adoniram as he said in reply, "I assure you that I am as fully persuaded of the latter as of the former."

"Do you believe, then, that none but the disciples will be saved from sin and hell?"

"None but His disciples," affirmed Maung Shway-gnong.

"How then, can you remain, without taking the oath of allegiance to Jesus Christ, and becoming His full disciple, in body and soul?"

"It is my earnest desire to do so, by receiving baptism. For the very purpose of expressing that desire, I have come here today." The scholar looked Adoniram straight in the face.

"You say you are desirous of receiving baptism?" Adoniram's lips wavered even as he asked the all-important question. "May I ask *when* you desire to receive it?"

"At any time you will please to give it," announced Maung Shway-gnong. "Now—this moment, if you please," he added hopefully.

"Do you wish to receive baptism in public or in private?"

The scholar replied without hesitation. "I will receive

it at any time, and in any circumstances, that you please to direct."

Adoniram's face broke into a smile of thankfulness.

"Teacher," he said, his voice brimming with emotion, "I am satisfied, from your conversation this afternoon, that you are a true disciple. I reply, therefore, that I am as desirous of giving you baptism as you are of receiving it."

Everybody in the room was overjoyed. Ann, sick as she felt, had already risen from her bed and joined them. In turn Adoniram looked at each of the happy faces surrounding him. There between the thin walls of the little mission he stood amidst strong friends. Beyond stretched the eternal darkness, with all its dangers, that was Burma. He recalled then the immortal words of John Bunyan:

> *Who so beset him round*
> *With dismal stories,*
> *Do but themselves confound—*
> *His strength the more is.*
> *No foes shall stay his might,*
> *Though he with giants fight;*
> *He will make good his right*
> *To be a pilgrim.*

Fortified and encouraged by the amazing conversion he had just witnessed, Adoniram asked another man in the company, Maung Thay-ay, "Are you, too, willing to take the oath of allegiance to Jesus Christ?"

Maung Thay-ay began to fidget nervously. He tried to look at Maung Shway-gnong out of one eye and at Adoniram with the other. At last he blurted, "If the teacher Maung Shway-gnong consents, why should I hesitate?"

This answer did not exactly please Adoniram.

"And if he does not consent, what then?" he asked.

160

"Then I must wait a little longer," was the answer.

"Stand by," said Adoniram, his face flushing. "You trust in Maung Shway-gnong, rather than in Jesus Christ. You are not worthy of being baptized."

Maung Thay-ay's face fell and he stepped back into the shadows. Then Adoniram saw how intently Ann was looking at her friend Mah Men-lay. Perhaps the Burmese woman was ready to join the scholar in baptism. Quietly he asked her, but she replied, "If the teacher thinks it suitable for me to be baptized, I am desirous of receiving baptism." Again Adoniram was not satisfied.

Next evening at dusk with a soft breeze blowing in from the river Adoniram baptized Maung Shway-gnong in the yellowish brown waters of the pond with the giant statue of the Buddha looking benignly down as ever. Mah Men-lay, her arm supporting the sick Ann, whispered to her friend, "Ah! He has gone to obtain the command of Jesus Christ, while I remain without obeying. I shall not be able to sleep this night. I must go home and consult my husband."

Adoniram and Ann were hardly settled in bed when they were awakened by an excited Mah Men-lay begging to be baptized that very moment. Overjoyed, the Judsons struggled back into their day clothes and accompanied Mah Men-lay through the dark silent streets to the waters of the pool. There, with Ann holding the lantern, Adoniram baptized the first Burmese woman into the Christian faith. She made the tenth member of his Burmese church.

Afterwards in the mission house Mah Men-lay said to Ann, "Now I have taken the oath of allegiance to Jesus Christ; and I have nothing to do but to commit myself, soul and body, into the hands of my Lord, assured that He will never suffer me to fall away."

seventeen

"C̲ome back; come back soon." A crowd of Burmese nearly a hundred strong, with countless naked little children, their lips dripping with red betel, lined the river bank as the boat cast off, taking the Judsons to the waiting ship. The women were crying aloud.

"Oh, if only we did not have to go," Ann repeated over and over.

It was August 18, 1820, when they reached Calcutta. Ann immediately underwent treatment from a Doctor Chalmers who gallantly refused payment. He believed her malady to be a chronic ailment of the liver. Sadly she heard the verdict: a return to Rangoon would be courting certain death. He thought that a period spent in the cooler climate of her native land might help. Then another eminent physician, a Doctor Macwhirter, prescribed medicines that would enable her to accompany Adoniram back to Burma. She was overjoyed. On November 23, back to Rangoon they sailed with Emily Van Someren. It was a stormy passage, their ship, the *Salamanca*, taking six instead of the expected two weeks. Never had the three passengers encountered such terrible thunderstorms. On the open sea it seemed impossible that the solitary ship could escape the flashes of lightning.

At the river mouth leading to Rangoon the pilot who came aboard to guide the *Salamanca* had a great deal of information to give them. Their old friends Mya-day-men and his wife were back in the city, the spear-stalker again being viceroy. This greatly pleased the Judsons, but the news that troops numbering thirty thousand men had recently marched through Rangoon en route to make war on Siam was very disturbing.

Maung Shway-gnong had escaped the persecution as a Buddhist scholar turned Christian that he had expected. The return to Rangoon of the old viceroy had thwarted the Mangen Teacher's conspiracy to obtain his downfall. When Mya-day-men was told, "The teacher Maung Shway-gnong is trying to turn the bottom of the priests' rice pot upwards," he snapped irritably, "What consequence? Let the priests turn it back again."

Waiting at the wharf was an excited group of the Judsons' own beloved disciples led by Mah-Men-lay. There were many eager hands to help them through the usual involved custom proceedings. Then triumphantly everybody returned to the mission, delighted at "Mrs. Yoodthan's" apparent recovery to health.

The vicereine desired to see her friend Ann without

delay. With feminine pride she told how she had received from the Golden Presence himself the marvelous title of Woon-gyee-gau-dau, a name and position similar to that of a Duchess. She was now allowed to ride in a *wau*, carried by fifty men. The viceroy, she explained, was sad over the death of his favorite daughter, one of the King's wives. She had said little when her husband strode in. "Ah! You are come!" he exclaimed, pointing at Ann with his spear before marching out again.

Ann's other friend, the gentle Mah Men-lay, had her own special surprise for "Mrs. Yoodthan," for she was about to open a school for boys so that they would not have to visit the Buddhist priests for instruction.

A steady flow of inquirers now streamed into the mission, encouraged by the Burmese disciples who themselves were spreading the message of Christ. Adoniram was busy translating again, but now he had the scholar Maung Shway-gnong to help him. The Gospel according to Saint Matthew and the first part of the Book of Acts, together with the Epistle to the Ephesians, were already done. George Hough would have plenty of copy to feed his printing press now set up in Serampore.

By mid-July Adoniram had translated both the Gospel and Epistles of Saint John, to be followed by the rest of Acts. No single day seemed long enough; often he thought a man needed several lifetimes to accomplish all the tasks he had set himself.

When fever struck both the Judsons helpless, thirteen-year-old Emily nursed them both with great devotion. During her years at the mission she had grown mature in mind and ways far beyond her natural years. Adoniram slowly recovered but the fever had brought on Ann's old liver complaint with new intensity. Even courses of salivation and Dr. Macwhirter's blue mercury pills failed to have the desired effect. Adoniram knew she must return to Bengal and possibly even America.

As could be expected, Ann dreaded the separation from her husband. She was near tears when on August 21, 1822, she sailed with her "little Emily" for Calcutta. From there the Dutch girl would journey on to her former home in Madras. Ann believed that the foster daughter she had come to love was destined to be a teacher. Already she could visualize Emily instructing a class of Indian boys and girls.

Adoniram was just as heartbroken at losing Ann. In a letter to George Hough written at the time of her departure he said, "I feel as if I was on the scaffold, and signing, as it were, my own death warrant . . . I have been occupied in making up my mind to have my right arm amputated, and my right eye extracted, which the doctors say are necessary in order to prevent a decay and mortification of the whole body conjugal."

The impulsive, self-assured missionary by this time admitted in letters written to friends in America that Ann, or Nancy as he sometimes familiarly called her, was his own right arm and eye.

Ann's ship was hardly at sea before she became violently ill, never expecting to reach Calcutta alive. During that time she experienced the dreadful nightmares of dying at sea. Perhaps these fears harked back to the time her brother John was lost in the deep, for Ann's worst dream was to die and be wrapped in a winding sheet and cast into the ocean. Once more Emily acted as sick-nurse. "Truly," Ann thought as she lay tossing in her bunk, "this is an exceptional child."

Arriving somewhat recovered in Calcutta, Ann bade Emily a fond farewell, having a premonition she would never see her again. Emily felt the same way. All her long life she never forgot her foster mother. Even as an old woman she would recall the smiling, curly-haired woman in whom she had placed her childhood faith.

The doctors were firm. Only a voyage to a cool climate would benefit Mrs. Judson. Naturally Ann preferred to visit her parents in America, but a search among the American ships was very disappointing. Their captains all said they had full cargoes, although one generously offered to take her home for fifteen hundred rupees. "But I could not think of causing the Board so great an expense," she said.

It was then suggested that she might take the long journey to England as a tonic for her health. Mrs. Thomason, wife of the East India Company's chaplain, discovered a "pious captain" who would take Ann to England for only five hundred rupees, if she would not mind sharing a cabin with three children. The offer was gratefully accepted. Later Ann found that the children's father had insisted on paying for her passage.

On going aboard she wrote to Dr. Thomas Baldwin in Boston,

If the pain in my side is entirely removed while on my passage to Europe, I shall return to India in the same ship, and proceed immediately to Rangoon. But if not, I shall go over to America, and spend one winter in my dear native country. As ardently as I long to see my beloved friends in America, I cannot prevail on myself to be any longer from Rangoon than is absolutely necessary for the preservation of life.

In her journal she confided her most personal inner thoughts at this time of parting from her beloved Adoniram. In it she wrote,

Those only who have been through a variety of toil and privation, to obtain a darling object can realize how entirely every fibre of the heart adheres to that object when secured. Had we encountered no difficulties, and suffered no privations in our attempts to form a church of Christ, under the government of a heathen despot, we should have been warmly attached to the individuals composing it, but should not have felt that tender solicitude and anxious affection, as in the present case.

Rangoon, from having been the theatre, in which so much of the faithfulness, power and mercy of God had been exhibited—from having been considered, for ten years past, as my home for life—and from a thousand interesting associations of ideas, had become the dearest spot on earth. Hence you will readily imagine that no ordinary consideration could have induced my departure.

She and Adoniram together had sunk alien New England roots securely into their exotic new environment. Leaving Burma now meant leaving home, while being parted from her husband became all the more distressing, knowing as she did that she might die on the journey or never be well enough to return.

Hardly had the ship put out to sea when Ann was subjected to another severe attack of her sickness. Everybody aboard was very kind to her. Two young English ladies of rank and influence were not only regular visitors but even administered to her physical needs. Later during her convalescence Ann read from her Bible "to help their minds." At other times she told them of her life in Burma, singing rice-pounding songs she had learned from the country women when they came down-river to visit relatives in the town. The two young ladies listened enthralled as Mrs. Judson sang,

> *Hey there, maiden at the loom,*
> *What cloth are you weaving?*
> *Oh, need you ask, in these thin times?*
> *It's a cotton coverlet for me.*
>
> *I live in a house of teak,*
> *Bright at night with torches.*
> *It's true, my parents are rich;*
> *Yet if you dare not come yourself,*
> *You can at least send a letter.*

Then with a sly dash of the mischievous Ann Hasseltine of old she would pretend to shock her English friends as she continued,

> *The poor man is moping in the house*
> *Feeling out of sorts and shaky*
> *Because he's short of opium.*
> *Very well, wry topknot,*
> *Sell my fine gold earplugs if you must,*
> *And make sure you get a good price for them!*
>
> *My handsome brother, a word with you*
> *Before you leave for lower country;*
> *If you find a wife there do not leave her,*
> *Bring her to us, we've use for her.*
> *She can fetch us water, gather firewood,*
> *And pound our rice—oh, lots of uses!*

The British were very kind to Ann. On arrival in England she discovered herself to be rather a celebrity. The eminent Joseph Butterworth, Member of Parliament and a leading Methodist, immediately invited her to stay in his home. There she received several distinguished visitors, including William Wilberforce, the philanthropist and abolitionist, William Babington, the philosopher; and Somers, the King of England's own chaplain.

Mr. Butterworth was delighted with his guest. Later at a meeting of the English Baptist Missionary Society he declared that her visit reminded him of the apostolic admonition, *Be not forgetful to entertain strangers for thereby some have entertained angels unawares.*

Ann's expenses while in the British Isles were paid by well-wishers from various Christian denominations. She visited Cheltenham to drink the famed health-giving mineral waters and then accepted an invitation to stay in Scotland. There she received a letter from the Baptist Mission Board in America suggesting that she leave at once for the United States on the New York packet.

Hurriedly traveling by stagecoach to the port of Liverpool, she found a band of charitable women in that city who insisted on giving her a passage on a larger and more comfortable ship. On August 16, 1822, she set sail on the *Amity.* Her journal entry for the day reads:

Should I be preserved through the voyage, the next land I tread will be my own native soil, ever loved America, the land of my birth. I cannot realize that I shall ever again find myself in my own dear home at Bradford amid the scenes of my early youth, where every spot is associated with some tender recollection. But the constant idea that my husband is not a participator of my joys will mar them all.

Ann left England feeling decidedly better in health, convinced that a spell in her native air would complete the cure. Arriving on September 25 in New York, she found the dreaded yellow fever prevalent there and immediately boarded a steamboat for Philadelphia, where she rested for a few days before taking the stagecoach to her parents' home in Bradford.

How slowly the horses seemed to go. Even the brilliance of the New England fall could not distract her mind from the reunion ahead.

Deacon and Mrs. Hasseltine welcomed their daughter as if from the dead. Mary and Abigail, Ann's sisters, were there, the latter now the popular preceptress of Bradford Academy, the pride of all the community. Hundreds of well-meaning neighbors and strangers poured into the white frame house to pay their respects, and nobody seemed to realize that so much strain and excitement were almost killing their heroine, who for six weeks did not enjoy a single night of undisturbed sleep.

One day Ann addressed the pupils at her sister's academy. It was a proud moment for Abigail Hasseltine as the youngsters listened entranced to Ann's description of Burma.

At last Elnathan Judson, Adoniram's brother, now employed by the government as a surgeon in Baltimore, realized the danger the prolonged welcome was having on his frail sister-in-law's health. He wisely insisted on taking her back to spend the winter in warmer Maryland.

Lightly referring to her condition as "my Indian constitution," she joined him December 3 at his boarding house. It had not been easy leaving her old home at Bradford again, but always the purpose uppermost in her mind was a quick recovery so that she might return to Adoniram in Rangoon.

In Baltimore she took more treatments of salivation with mercury. Elnathan saw that she was attended by the best physicians in the city who all agreed that a fierce New England winter would have killed her. From her sickroom she began work on a book that Mr. Butterworth, the British Member of Parliament, had urged her to write describing the Burmese mission. This she wrote in the form of a collection of letters addressed to him personally and entitled *An Account of the American Mission to the Burman Empire, in a Series of Letters Addressed to a Gentleman in London.* She journeyed to Washington to proof-read her book and confer with a committee appointed by the Baptist General Convention. The book was published in London in 1823. During the same year it came out in Washington under the title *A Particular Relation of the American Baptist Mission to the Burman Empire.* During this busy period Ann found time to sit for an oil portrait by the prominent artist Rembrandt Peale.*

Ann's wearing apparel did not go unnoticed by other women during her American visit. It was rumored that in ways of dress the famed woman missionary was extremely extravagant and the Baptists felt obliged to publish the following document:

CIRCULAR

VINDICATION OF MRS. JUDSON

The Committee appointed by the Boston Baptist Association, at Salem, Sept. 18th, 1823, to take into consideration the reports which have been circulated concerning the

* In this most beautiful surviving likeness of Mrs. Judson she is seen wearing a gown of soft lavender blue given her by sympathetic British admirers. Today the portrait hangs at historic 24 West Cedar Street, Boston, the home of Miss Lillian Watson, adopted daughter of Frances Vose Emerson whose family were related to the same Reverend Joseph Emerson who married Ann's sister, Rebecca Hasseltine.

172

extravagance of Mrs. Judson's dress, and to publish the result of their inquiries, beg leave to make the following statements.

In a newspaper published in this city on the 25th of July last, the following communication appeared, and has been since transcribed into other papers:

"Mrs. Judson, the wife of A. Judson, a famous missionary in the East Indies, sailed from Boston, a short time since, where she had been, to visit her friends, and collect MONEY from the pious and charitable to aid her in distributing the bread of life to the poor heathen of Asia. A lady, who was in habits of familiar intercourse with Mrs. Judson, and to whom application was made for charity, in her behalf, informs us, that the *visiting dress* of this *self-denying* female missionary could not be valued at less than TWELVE HUNDRED DOLLARS!! The reader may be startled at the mention of such an enormous amount laid out in a *single* dress to decorate the person of one whose affections are professedly set on heavenly things, and despising the vain and gaudy allurements of the world; it appeared to us incredible, till we heard from the lady some of the details. The *cashmere shawl* was valued at $600; the *Leghorn Flat* $150; lace trimming on the gown $150, &c.; jewelry would soon make up the sum, leaving *necessary* articles of clothing out of the question. We hope the next edition of the missionary arithmetic, will inform us how many infants were robbed of their innocent, if not necessary playthings, how many widows had denied themselves the use of sugar in tea and butter on bread, how many poor debtors had robbed their creditors and laboured without stockings and shoes, to furnish out this modern representative of the mystical Babylon."

173

The personal friends of Mrs. Judson read this communication with surprise and sorrow, mingled with feelings of just indignation. They knew that a difference of opinion existed as to the reasonableness and utility of Foreign Missions, but they did not expect, that the character of a female, who was laboring under the pressure of bodily indisposition, would be unnecessarily assailed.

It was a knowledge of this fact which led to the appointment of the aforesaid Committee by the Boston Baptist Association.

Soon after the publication of the above statement, Mr. E. Lincoln waited on the Editor and requested to be introduced to the lady who was in "habits of familiar intercourse with Mrs. Judson, and to whom application was made for charity in her behalf"; and who had informed him, that the *visiting dress* of this *self-denying* female Missionary could not be valued at less than twelve hundred dollars. The Editor introduced him to the gentleman who authorized the communication. This gentleman referred him to his Mother, as the lady alluded to in the above named news-paper. Mr. Lincoln therefore called on her, and was surprised to learn, that this lady, "in habits of familiar intercourse with Mrs. Judson," had never seen her; that she had never been applied to for charity in her behalf; and had no personal knowledge respecting any item in the communication. She stated to Mr. Lincoln that she had received her information from another lady, whom she named. Mr. Lincoln then sought an interview with this person, who it was said had boarded in the same house with Mrs. Judson, and had seen her rich dresses. But she declared to him, that she had never boarded in the same house, and had never seen either Mrs. Judson, or her apparel; but had heard the statement from a lady, who had received it from another lady in Bradford; a small town about thirty miles from this city.

The Committee now state, that the articles of dress, of which so much has been said, were not purchased, either with the private property of Mrs. Judson, or with Missionary Money; but were presented to her by different individuals as tokens of personal affection and respect. The Cashmere

Shawl, "valued at $600," was given to her in England by the sister of a distinguished friend of Missions; and we are assured from very respectable authority that it cost twenty-five dollars. "The *Leghorn flat* valued at $150," was purchased in Salem; and from the certain knowledge of two ladies concerned in the purchase, did not exceed in its cost, eight dollars and fifty cents. As to the Lace trimming on the gown, stated at $150, a very *intimate friend* at whose house Mrs. Judson stayed, says, "she had not to my knowledge, one gown that had a particle of lace upon it. If she had I was ignorant of it, or it was so trifling, that it did not make an impression sufficient to be remembered." We feel authorized to state, from the testimony of other ladies of unquestionable veracity, who visited with Mrs. Judson in different cities, and who saw the apparel in her possession, that this is a just representation.

Concerning what is said of her jewelry, which, in order to make up the aforesaid sum of $1200, is estimated at $300, we scarcely know how to express ourselves. With the exception of a chain, and a small locket in which was the likeness of one of the family, and these were given her, it is believed that all her jewelry was not worth five dollars.

For the information of those who did not see Mrs. Judson while she was in this country, the Committee would remark, that a majority of them had the pleasure of receiving her into their families as a guest: and the impression left on their minds was, that she had a soul too elevated to be occupied in ornamenting her person. She was in fact, distinguished for the plainness and cheapness of dress.

The same individuals met with her frequently in the cities of New York and Washington; but in no instance did they see anything in her deportment or apparel, which did not accord with that modesty, simplicity and plainness which becometh women professing godliness.

Having stated these facts, the Committee deem it unnecessary to offer any comment upon them, but would leave each reader to make his own reflections.

It may be proper to state, that the Committee are in possession of the names of all the parties concerned, but as the mention of them did not seem necessary for the defence of our highly esteemed friend, Mrs. Judson, they are from motives of delicacy suppressed.

Signed in behalf and by order of the Boston Baptist Association,

THOMAS BALDWIN
LUCIUS BOLLES
DANIEL SHARP
GEORGE KEELY,
Boston, Oct. 1, 1823.   ENSIGN LINCOLN

Winter passed and with much improved health Ann returned in late spring to her beloved Bradford. From there she made quick trips to Salem, Charlestown, Cambridge, Saugus and Plymouth. On June 22 she sailed from Boston accompanied by Mr. and Mrs. Jonathan Wade, who were to work with the Burmese mission. As the ship slowly sailed out of Boston Harbor on that warm summer's day, Ann Hasseltine Judson compared it with the bitterly cold morning in 1812 when she had previously set out for Burma. This time, however, there was a difference: she was going back to Adoniram and their home.

eighteen

When Ann first left Rangoon Adoniram worked hard at his translation as a solace for her absence. Mya-day-men the viceroy and his friendly wife promised they would try to speak to the King of toleration when he passed through Rangoon on his way to direct the attack on Siam. To them freedom of worship meant freedom for foreigners only. They did not seem to comprehend that any fellow Burmese had dared to embrace a new religion.

The baptism of the scholar Maung Shway-gnong could not be kept secret. In no time the viceroy received the damning news of his "having embraced sentiments which aimed at the destruction of the Boodhist religion, and prejudicial to the existing authorities." There was nothing the viceroy could do but agree that if such a statement were true then Maung Shway-gnong should face execution. But he did nothing about arresting the culprit, allowing him time to get his family and himself safely up river to the town of Shway-doung about a hundred miles away, taking along a good supply of Adoniram's translations of the scriptures.

About this time Maung Thahlah, the second Christian convert and brother of the quarrelsome Mah Baik, died of cholera.

On December 13, 1821, Dr. and Mrs. Jonathan Price with their baby daughter arrived at the mission. Price, whose studies in medicine had been paid for by the Baptist Board, proved in one way a very great source of irritation to the meticulous Adoniram who of course was obliged to share his home with the newcomers. Doctor or not, Jonathan Price hadn't the slightest concept of neatness or cleanliness.

The inhabitants of Rangoon were certain that a magician had come to dwell in their midst, for the sandy-haired doctor could remove a cataract from the eye as easily as most people peel a banana. He had quickly established a successful practice as a doctor, parrotlike picking up the language. The Burmese were delighted. Soon news of Dr. Price and his magical powers found their way to the Golden Ears. Price was ordered to make an official visit (all expenses paid) to Ava.

Before he could do so his wife had died of the dysentery. They buried her beside little Roger in the grove of mango trees, and the baby was sent back to Calcutta to be properly looked after. On August 20 another death occurred—Mya-day-men the viceroy. Then to everyone's surprise the Houghs arrived again in Rangoon with their printing press.

On August 27 Price left for Ava, accompanied by a rather reluctant Adoniram who deplored being diverted, at this

178

crucial point, from his daily task of translating the Bible. His great desire was to get this colossal work finished, for he knew himself to be the only person then able to do it.

Unlike the previous unsuccessful visit to the capital, there were no obstacles this time to obtaining an audience. Dressed in his old-fashioned black suit, Adoniram attended Dr. Price in the secondary rôle of interpreter. Although Price could make himself understood, Adoniram's command of the Burmese language would be more readily understandable to the Golden Ears. As was the custom with each new king, Bagyidaw had moved the Golden City to an entirely new location. During the rebuilding, which was still in progress, over forty thousand houses had actually been moved from the old site at Amarapura.

The King was in good humor the day of the audience but the Golden Eyes were only for Price. They did not seem to notice Adoniram at all or recognize him as one of the two men who, dressed in spotless white, had appeared on that other ill-fated occasion. Fortunately the Atwinwun Maung Zah did. He courteously inquired after Adoniram's health and well-being, and then suggested that it might be good to remain some little time in the Golden City.

On the first day of October they were again summoned to the Golden Presence, and this time the King deigned to notice Adoniram.

"And you, in black," he demanded, "what about you? Are you a medical man too?"

"Not a medical man," replied Adoniram, "but a teacher of religion, Your Majesty."

"Have any embraced your religion?" The question so surprised Adoniram that his heart seemed to give an extra beat.

"Not here in Ava," he replied, but such an evasive answer did not satisfy the curious king.

"Are there any in Rangoon?" he asked.

"There are a few." Adoniram felt hot under his white linen neckcloth.

"Are there any foreigners?"

There was no escape. He would speak the truth and hope for the best. His voice shook as he answered, "There are some foreigners and some Burmans."

There was deep silence. None of the Burmese present in the audience chamber stirred from their prostrate positions. Then the Golden Lips moved to discuss cosmography and astrology! Adoniram breathed with relief, for the King now knew that some of his own subjects had become Christians, yet had not lost his temper.

It seemed they would be detained at Ava for some time because the King wished to know more of Price and his magical powers. This provided Adoniram with a good opportunity to cultivate a number of friendships close to the royal court. Most important of these was his contact with the eldest half-brother of the King, whom Adoniram always referred to as "Prince M." He was an invalid, his legs and arms so weak and twisted they were all but useless. Twenty-eight years old and married to the King's sister, the Princess of Sarawady, he possessed a brilliant mind. Describing his special interest to be "foreign science," he hoped Adoniram could enlighten him.

Adoniram visited the home of Prince M. and his wife on several occasions. To the princess he presented a copy of Ann's little catechism, which she courteously accepted although her husband seemed little interested in religion. Once he even remarked that he did not think his brother would persecute any Burmese who became Christians, declaring, "He has a good heart and he wishes all people to believe and worship as they please."

Astronomy, not religion, was a subject much more to his taste, although the theory advanced by the American teacher that the earth and planets revolved around the sun was something he refused to believe. At the same time he found himself unable to reason with Adoniram on these points.

The prince and princess began to enjoy the regular visits of Adoniram. If the King did not want to lose Price, they felt equally possessive of his friend. "Do not return to Rangoon," they begged him. "When your wife arrives, call her to Ava. The King will give you a piece of ground on which to build a *kyoung*." A *kyoung* was a house for holy people to reside in.

Adoniram was no fool. With the contacts he had made among the royal family there was no limit to what he might achieve for his mission. He was impatient for Ann to return, for she was particularly good at winning friends. He could see now that it would not be a mistake to present her at the Golden Court.

At last he felt himself in a position to speak frankly of Christianity to Prince M. Adoniram described his own conversion, then implored the crippled prince to search his own mind for the truth before it was too late. The prince sighed, for he genuinely liked the American teacher and did not wish to offend him.

"I am young yet, only twenty-eight," he answered. "I want to study all the foreign arts and sciences. Then my mind will be enlarged, and I will be able to judge whether the Christian religion will be true or not."

"But suppose your Highness changes worlds in the meantime?" countered Adoniram, his eyes purposely wandering to the cushions upon which the unfortunate cripple was propped.

"It is true, I do not know when I shall die," agreed the prince with the quiet acceptance of one who has lived close to death so long that any fears had long since lost their sting.

"Pray to God for light," begged Adoniram. "If you receive light you will be able at once to distinguish between truth and falsehood."

In addition to the prince and princess, some of the nobles and even Atwinwuns desired to cultivate Adoniram's friendship. The Golden Presence commanded a small house to be built next to the wall surrounding Prince M.'s home for Dr. Price and Adoniram. Things continued to go well, while from Rangoon news came that this time George Hough the printer seemed more adjusted to life in Burma. They received the sad information that young Colman had died in Chittagong, so the prospect of having an alternative location for a mission was now nonexistent. The sensible thing was to remain in Ava.

There was also the question of the *kyoung* suggested by Prince M. and his wife. The Golden Presence was approached and his permission obtained on the condition that Adoniram could first find a piece of unoccupied ground.

This was enough for Adoniram Judson. Losing no time, he looked diligently until he came upon a desirable site for the *kyoung*. He called in the Royal Measurer who in turn told the all-powerful Atwinwuns that the chosen spot was sacred, having once been the location of another *kyoung*. Shrugging his shoulders, the King decreed impatiently, "Well, give him some vacant spot."

On one special occasion, when Adoniram was with Dr. Price and two Englishmen who were visiting the capital, the Golden Eyes even singled him out. The four made a strange little group as, minus their shoes, they sat cross-legged in European clothes.

King Bagyidaw strode toward them and then stopped, pointing a finger at Adoniram. "Concerning those who have embraced your religion, are they real Burmans?" he demanded.

"Oh, yes, Your Majesty," Adoniram said with a nod.

"Do they dress like other Burmans?"

"Yes, they are just like all the other Burmese."

Then Adoniram told of how on his own Holy Day he preached in the Christian *zayat* at Rangoon.

"What! In Burmese?" The King was a little taken back.

"Yes," replied Adoniram.

The King rubbed his hands in anticipation. "Let us hear how you preach."

Adoniram could hardly believe his own ears. The Golden Presence actually wanted to hear *him* preach? Slowly, in a quiet voice, Adoniram began:

"God is a spirit, without bodily form. Although omnipresent, it is above the heavens that He clearly discovers His glory. His power and wisdom are infinite. He is pure and good, and possessed of everlasting felicity."

The King listened intently, and so did his courtiers, as the foreign teacher enumerated the high aims and aspirations of a true Christian:

"Suppress haughtiness, pride and insolence, and cherish a humble, meek and lowly mind. Return not evil for evil, but have a disposition to forgive the faults of others. Love your enemies and pray for them. Be compassionate to the poor and needy, and give alms. Covet not the property of others; therefore, take not by violence, steal not, defraud not in trade. Trespass not on the property of others. Speak no falsehood. Before this world was made God remained happy, surrounded by the pure and incorporeal sons of heaven. In order to display His perfections, and make creatures happy, God created the heavens, the sun, moon, and

183

all the stars, the earth, the various kinds of brute creatures, and man."

The Golden Hand was raised. The Golden Ears had heard all that they wanted to hear. Loyally the Golden Lips inquired from the foreign teacher his opinion of the Buddha. Adoniram carefully worded his reply for he had no wish to offend the King.

"We all know that he was the son of King Thog-dau-daunah. We regard him as a wise man and a great teacher. But we do not call him God." Adoniram bowed his head.

At that moment, quite forgetting his manners, an Atwinwun shouted in a loud voice, "That is right. The Christian idea is that there is only one Being Who exists eternally, and how there are Three united in One: God the Father, God the Son, and God the Holy Ghost."

"Nearly all the world, Your Majesty," ventured Maung Zah, "believes in an eternal God. All except Burma and Siam, those little spots!"

For some moments after this surprising outburst the Golden Lips remained closed. Suddenly they opened to inquire after the health of Adoniram Judson's wife.

A few days later Adoniram informed the Golden Ears he would be returning to Rangoon. "Will you go from there to your own country?" asked the Golden Lips.

"Only to Rangoon."

"Will you both go, or will the doctor remain?" Maung Zah the Atwinwun was speaking.

Adoniram told them Price would be staying, and that in time he himself hoped to return. The King was pleased, for he did not want to lose the medical services of Price. "Let a place be given him," he declared.

Later that evening Maung Zah surprised Adoniram by saying, "Gaudama and Christ and Mahomet, and others, are great teachers, who communicated as much truth respectively as they could; but their communications are not the word of God. This is a deep and difficult subject. So you, teacher, consider further, and I also will consider."

At last Adoniram found a piece of land to his liking on which to erect the *kyoung*, but to his annoyance saw that the chief Wungyi had already fenced it in for a private *zayat* of his own. Perhaps he could make the Wungyi change his mind. For days Adoniram pursued him with both a written petition and money for a bribe. At last he managed to get them safely into the Wungyi's hands, hopefully waiting while he pocketed the bribe and read the petition.

The Wungyi apparently thought it would be stupid to give in to the foreign teacher so easily, when there might be another gift forthcoming. "You are indefatigable in your search for a place," he told the eager Adoniram, "but you cannot have that. It is for my own use. Search further."

Adoniram, though disappointed, was far from feeling despondent. Following the Wungyi like a shadow, one evening he found him "lying down, surrounded by forty or fifty people." This time he had a bottle of perfume for the gift-loving official which was obviously to his taste for he inquired, looking up, "What kind of house do you intend to build?"

Adoniram explained that it would be small, just large enough for his wife and himself, adding wistfully, "But I have no place to build on, my lord."

The Wungyi took a long sniff at the pleasing perfume; then, feeling benevolent in the presence of so many guests, he announced, "If you want the little enclosure, take it." Adoniram gratefully thanked him, but this was insufficient for the Wungyi. Here was good entertainment for his guests. Let the foreign teacher preach as he had done the other day before the Golden Presence. The missionary was only too pleased to oblige. He preached until the Wungyi was so tired of listening that he fell back on his cushions with exhaustion.

Next evening he brought the Wungyi the purchase money, feeling disturbed when he refused to take it, until the official explained, "Understand, teacher, that we do not give you the entire owning of this ground. We take no recompense, lest it become American territory. We give it to you for your present residence only; and when you go, we shall take it again."

Adoniram was satisfied, although he tried to extract the further promise that if he had a missionary successor, that man could occupy it also.

In two short days the neat house of bamboo and teak was completed. A disciple would live there while Adoniram was absent in Rangoon. Promising to translate all of the Scriptures, he bade farewell to his good friends the prince and princess. On January 25, 1823, the foreign teacher left Ava to collect all his household goods and chattels and—he hoped—his wife.

nineteen

Tabaung with all its many festivities came and went; the Burmese year was ending. The scarlet blossoms of the butea fell upon the dusty ground. This was the time that Ann liked best of all in Burma, Adoniram kept remembering. Would she never return?

The air was sweet with the fragrant ingyin growing in a neighboring compound; he watched the last of the red cotton tree petals as they faded and disappeared. Then came April and New Year. He heard the happy shouting of the young folk as they passed by, scattering the aged with scented water as a mark of respect. This was Thingyan the Water Festival. As he walked through the city he often came upon groups of happy, dancing Burmese. How na-

187

turally the poetic movements of body and feet seemed to suit them. Nostalgically he thought of the honeymoon voyage with Ann to Burma. They had called it the "long honeymoon." How invigorating then their dancing had been.

In early May came the full moon of Kason when the people recalled the enlightenment of the Buddha as he sat beneath the bo tree on the great plain by the Ganges River. The people filled Pagoda Road on their way to the mighty Shwe-Dagon Pagoda carrying offerings of uncooked rice, fruit and little jars of oil. Adoniram's eardrums ached from the continual joyous striking of gongs and cymbals.

Then came the monsoon, as it came every year. All at once the heavens seemed to break open, the rain pouring in rivers over the mud-baked roads. The mission house was depressing with the continual flow of water beating monotonously upon the roof. While the gift-laden faithful continued to jostle their way through the drenching downpour to the golden pagoda, Adoniram kept to his study where he completed the translation of the whole New Testament together with a twelve-section summary of the Old. With so much work accomplished he could be forgiven his impatience over the fact that George Hough could not continue printing until new type arrived from Bengal.

The mission had deteriorated while Adoniram was in Ava. Several disciples had been denounced as Christians by their neighbors and their homes destroyed. One of them, a woman named Mah Myat-ya, had even lost her life. When Adoniram asked her sister how she had died he was told that Mah Myat-ya had not been afraid; she had put her whole trust in Jesus Christ.

One of the converts, Maung Shway-bay, decided to write a letter to Dr. Thomas Baldwin in Boston, which Adoniram delighted in translating. Calling Dr. Baldwin "Beloved Elder Brother," the Burmese told him,

Though in the present state the places of our residence are very far apart, and we have never met, yet by means of letters, and of the words of Yoodthan, who has told me of you, I love you and wish to send you this letter.

In this country of Burmah are many strayed sheep. Teacher Yoodthan, pitying them, has gone to gather them together, and to feed them in love. Some will not listen, but run away. Some do listen, and adhere to him; and that our number may increase, we meet together, and pray to the great proprietor of the sheep.

Thus I, Maung Shway-bay, a disciple of teacher Yoodthan in Rangoon, write and send this letter to the great teacher Baldwin who lives in Boston, America.

October came, and the Burmese springtime, feasting, dancing and the occasion of many weddings. The rain had stopped, the full moon of Thadingyut was shining in all its fair beauty. How he longed to hold Ann in his arms once more!

Then on December 5 she came.

They had been apart for twenty-seven months, yet when he caught his first glimpse of her Adoniram knew it had not been in vain. She looked so radiant and beautiful that he described her as "the Ann Hasseltine of other days." Also on the boat were the two new missionaries, Jonathan and Deborah Wade of Edinburgh, New York.

Ann actually felt better in health than did Adoniram, because of his frequent bouts of cholera, together with the burning sensation with which his eyes were so often afflicted.

At once Adoniram bundled the newly arrived Wades off to

the mission house which they would share with the Houghs,
Meanwhile Ann's luggage was transferred to a boat waiting in the river. There was no time to argue, no need for
her to stay any longer than was necessary at the mission
house with that sad little grave out in the compound.
Proudly, like a knight of old, he was at last taking her to
the Golden City of Ava.

Happily she showed him the new rocker and work table
given her by his brother Elnathan in Baltimore. They were
loaded for the journey, together with other small furnishings
from the mission. Ann was thankful she had advised Mrs.
Wade to come well supplied with things of her own.

Maung Ing, the fisherman convert, and the Bengali cook,
whom Ann had managed to talk into leaving his native
surroundings, would accompany them. A week later the
party set out for Ava, prepared to spend Christmas Day
on the water. The Judsons had plenty of time for talking
during the river trip; they both had so many things to ask
each other. For him there were countless questions regarding their respective families in America, while she had to
catch up on all that had happened during her absence from
Burma. There was only one cloud to shadow their horizon;
this time, after so many years of rumor, war with the
British seemed about to begin.

Ann had been told by the chief secretary of the Bengal
Government in Calcutta that to return to Rangoon at such
a time was sheer foolishness. There had been a number of
recent border incidents which the British could not ignore,
although they did not particularly want war. The Burmese
had opened fire on British civilians sailing on the Naaf
River; they had also attacked a British outpost on the isle
of Shahpuri. Lord Amherst the Governor General had protested, but in this very protest the Burmese thought they
smelt weakness. Finally they kidnapped two British naval

190

officers whom they had invited to discuss the border troubles.

Surprisingly the British failed to grasp the ignorance of the Burmese concerning the strength of their "enemy." Burma regarded England as another Siam. With Siam captured, the riches of Bengal lay at their feet. Unlike the old king, Bagyidaw was at the mercy of his ministers. Maha Bandula, one of his generals, had grown so important that even the Golden Presence feared him.

In spite of such ugly forebodings the reunited missionaries determined to enjoy their journey as best they could, for being together again was cause enough to rejoice. Whenever their boat docked at a village they were immediately surrounded by crowds of excited people who had never before seen the face of a foreign woman. With her ready knowledge of Burmese, Ann joined in the fun. She understood all their remarks concerning her "strange" appearance, later writing, "all were anxious that their friends and relatives should have a view . . . some, who were less civilized than others, would run some way before us, in order to have a *long* look as we approached them."

Then at a place called Tsen-pyoo-kywon they discovered the encampment of Bandula's army of thirty thousand men. A little farther up-river the Judsons came face to face with a vast flotilla of golden warships accompanying the mighty barge carrying the great Bandula himself. It was a terrible moment, enough to try the most steel-like nerves. The warships with the high sterns where the helmsmen sat were each made from the enormous trunk of a teak tree. They were paddled by soldiers whose arms moved to the rhythm of stirring military music. The golden boats were filled with troops wearing simple black coatlike uniforms strengthened with linings of quilted cotton. There seemed no end to the rows of glittering spears and ominous muskets. Facing this fearsome array was the Judsons' one small boat.

In no time a golden warship was speeding toward them while Adoniram tried to think what excuse he was going to make for just happening to be on the river. His mind flashed back to the Golden Presence. Perhaps he was the answer.

The warship came alongside; the officer in charge demanded to know their business. Adoniram declared in as brave a voice as he could muster that they were on their way to Ava by no less than an order from the King himself. Besides, they were Americans, not English.

The investigating officer, satisfied by the simple explanation, immediately waved his hand, commanding the martial music to recommence. Wiping the sweat from his brow, Adoniram watched as the gleaming, snakelike ship slipped off to rejoin its fellows. Ann felt her heart beating naturally again.

On January 23, 1824, with Rangoon six weeks' journey behind them, the missionary boat docked a short distance below the new Ava. Dr. Price soon heard of their arrival and hurried out to greet them, but the news that followed was not pleasant, for foreigners were no longer welcome at the court. The Atwinwuns in power when Adoniram left Ava had been dismissed. Even Price and his magical medicine were out of favor. He advised the Judsons to remain in the brick house he had built for himself on the riverbank opposite the city. The house proved to be dripping with damp, and Ann had hardly set foot inside when she was taken with such severe chills followed by fever that Adoniram was obliged to take her back to the boat while a simple bamboo house was built for their own private use.

At this time a friendly visitor, if no longer an important one, arrived. The former vicereine, the spear-stalking Mya-day-men's widow, came aboard to greet Ann. With the death of her husband she had immediately been reduced to

192

the rank of an ordinary person. She accepted her humble position philosophically, with no misgivings. Together the two friends gossiped, sipped green tea and nibbled on pickled ginger. On leaving, the former vicereine gave Ann a tiny ivory fan decorated with orange flowers.

Adoniram visited the palace but the King was no longer interested in him. He took Ann to meet other members of the royal family but they gave little evidence of welcome; even the Queen had forgotten her desire to see the "foreign woman." Everyone's favorite topics were war and the splendid palace the King had built himself.

The royal family left for Amarapura, the former capital, only a few miles away, and their triumphal return in state for the dedication of the new palace is best described in Ann's own words:

I dare not attempt a description of that splendid day when majesty with all its attendant glory entered the gates of the golden city, and amid the acclamations of millions, I may say, took possession of the palace. The saupwars of the provinces bordering on China, all the viceroys and high officers of the kingdom, were assembled on the occasion, dressed in their robes of state, and ornamented with the insignia of their office. The white elephant, richly ornamented with gold and jewels, was one of the most beautiful objects in the procession. The king and queen alone were unadorned, dressed in the simple garb of the country; they hand in hand entered the garden in which we had taken our seats, and where a banquet was prepared for their refreshment. All the riches and glory of the empire were on this day exhibited to view. The number and immense size of the elephants, the numerous horses, and great variety of vehicles of all descriptions, far surpassed any thing I have ever seen or imagined.

With the court's return, the Golden Lips forbade all foreigners, with the exception of Lanciego the Spaniard,

Akoupwoon of Rangoon, from entering his wonderful golden palace. In spite of this unpleasantness the Judsons were not unhappy. Two weeks after Ann's arrival in Ava the small house of bamboo, raised by stilts some four feet from the ground, was finished. It was the best Adoniram could do at present, though he knew it would be brutal to live in during the scorching summer months. Already he was trying to obtain both bricks and masons to build for them a cooler structure.

Feeling fit and in good health again, Ann was bursting with energy. She lost no time in opening another small school with three little girls for her first pupils. The father of two of these, the same Maung Shway-bay who had written the delightfully sincere letter to Dr. Baldwin of Boston, wished Ann to become their foster mother, his wife being insane. She gladly consented, quickly naming them Mary Hasseltine and Abby Hasseltine after her own two sisters. Sending this news to her family in America she noted, "One of them is to be supported with the money which the 'Judson Association of Bradford Academy' have engaged to collect. They are fine children, and improve as rapidly as any children in the world."

Adoniram was also concerned with other things besides building a brick house. He was still translating, while on Sundays he crossed the river to preach at the home of Dr. Price. The precious New Testament manuscript was carefully guarded in readiness for printing.

Jonathan Price was not the most ideal colleague for Adoniram. Although Adoniram as a teacher of religion refused on principle to attend the Burmese boxing matches or sessions of elephant training, Price failed to deny himself such pleasures. While Adoniram had been away in Rangoon awaiting Ann's arrival the doctor had tried hard to win Imperial favor, once even entering the Golden Presence

194

without first being invited. The Golden Back had promptly turned itself upon the intruder.

Price had then operated on the eyes of a woman with the result that she lost what little sight remained. Although she was extremely ugly, in true cavalier style he decided to marry her, asking Adoniram to perform the ceremony. The missionary was disgusted, sensing that the true reason for the wedding was neither love nor pity but only to soothe the feelings of her Burmese relatives, already upset that because of him she had completely lost her sight.

"Brother Judson," declared Dr. Price, rather relishing the sight of Adoniram in such a predicament, "the law of America and of nature provides for cases where a minister is not to be found!" With this pointed reminder, Adoniram had to capitulate.

If Price's behavior disappointed the Judsons, there was another white man whose presence was some compensation. Every evening he would turn up at the bamboo mission house for tea and storytelling. Even Adoniram interrupted his studies when Henry Gouger the Englishman dropped in.

Gouger might be a rogue and very much a sinner, yet the Judsons discovered in him a sense of honesty and frankness sadly lacking in their own brother missionary. In return Gouger reconsidered his former distaste of missionaries in general. Now he thought that if religious organizations would send out young couples of the Judson caliber, then missionaries might prove a blessing in the Far East.

Henry Gouger was still only in his twenties when they first met him. Finding promotion in the East India Company too slow, he had invested in a ship and sailed for Ava, where his cheerful personality had immediately made him a great success with both King and nobility. The Burmese paid an enormous price in gold and precious stones for the goods he had to offer so that his fortune grew, yet under Burmese law he could take none of it out of the country. He might have been reimbursed with teak, but then there would have been no profit; transportation costs for shipping it overseas were immense.

Being a practical man, Henry Gouger had settled for the next best thing, deciding to stay and enjoy his new-found fortune on the spot. Wearing sandals and other items of Burmese clothing, he was also equipped with two servants named Red Rat and Red Gold. Like all Englishmen, Gouger liked his roast Sunday dinner, but in Burma where animals were protected by law from being killed for food, this presented a problem. They could only be eaten after natural or accidental death. More animals died of accidental death in Henry Gouger's compound at Ava than in the whole of Burma! He was of course always sure to send a generous portion of meat to those officials who otherwise might have felt rather uncomfortable on hearing of so many "accidents."

Until the time of the order denying foreigners the privilege of access to the palace Gouger had pleased the King very much, even acting as a horse for pulling the royal buggy, a gift from an English embassy. The Golden Presence preferred a team of men to horses.

Ann continued to teach, Adoniram to translate and build the brick house, and the Burmese—especially the womenfolk—to argue about the coming war. In discussing the English, the Prince of Sarawady, brother of the King, declared, "They have never yet fought with so strong and brave a people as the Burmans, skilled in the use of sword and spear." Neither he nor anybody else in Ava could imagine the English capable of defeating them.

On May 23, 1824, while Adoniram was conducting a service in the home of Dr. Jonathan Price, news was received that a British fleet had taken Rangoon by surprise, bombarded and captured it. That night Henry Gouger insisted on going home alone, for he recognized that as an Englishman he was a danger to his American friends. They must *not* meet.

The crafty Prince of Sarawady sent Gouger a message suggesting he should bring his wine, beer, silver and gold to his home for safety. Red Rat, Gouger's servant, smelt a human trap.

"Sahib," he said, "if the Prince were to know what I am going to tell you, my life would not be worth a day's purchase. This offer is only made that he may get you and his property in his power. You would then find a grave in his garden, as many persons have done before when it suited his purpose. He knows you have a great deal of gold and silver, and thinks he may as well get it as anyone else. When you came to be demanded by the Hlut-dau, [Council of State] as you would be, the only answer he could give would be that you had died, and there the matter might end. You will stand a better chance by remaining quiet and allowing yourself to be apprehended by the Wungyis, and disposed of according to their pleasure." Gouger declined the Prince of Sarawady's kind invitation.

Adoniram and Ann could only trust in God for their personal safety now that the long-expected war was a reality. They knew the Burmese either killed or enslaved prisoners-of-war. What would be their own lot they had no idea. From their windows they could see boatloads of soldiers sailing off down the yellow-gray waters of the Irrawaddy toward the combat area. The enthusiastic troops could not seem to wait to fight the English. Often the men were dancing when the boats passed the mission house. "Poor fellows, you will probably never dance again," Adoniram murmured as he watched them.

The loss of Rangoon did not unduly upset the Burmese,

197

for they thought the English had only sailed into what would eventually prove to be a delayed ambush. Many were even afraid that the fearful sight of Bandula's mighty army would make them take to their heels without even a fight. One nobleman begged an officer going to the front, "Bring me six white strangers to row my boat," while a hopeful middle-aged wife ordered, "Send me four white strangers to manage the affairs of my house, as I understand they are trusty servants." It was even rumored that Bandula had a pair of golden fetters ready to clamp on the legs of the governor general of Bengal when he should be brought back captive to Burma.

Then a surprising rumor trickled through the streets of the golden city of Ava: *All foreigners are spies.* The Burmese had good grounds for their suspicions in view of the various strangers who had lately been turning up in their capital. A pockmarked Scot named Captain Laird who had given cause for the Burmese king to ask if all Scots were as ugly as he, had been brought by force from Rangoon on orders issued by the Prince of Sarawady for whom he had been employed as teak agent. On his person Laird stupidly carried a Calcutta newspaper clipping containing information that the British planned to attack Rangoon. Foolishly he showed Henry Gouger the clipping and then translated the news to none other than the Prince of Sarawady himself.

For having withheld such vital information from the Golden Ears, Laird, Gouger and even Rodgers the Yorkshireman found themselves under arrest. Gouger, whose wealth made him a splendid prize for the greedy officials, was described by his accusers as being "brother-in-law to the East India Company." He was also charged with drawing maps of the country. Actually all he had drawn were simple sketches showing points of scenic interest.

Rodgers, the rival of Lanciego for the cherished collector-ship of Rangoon, was now quite out of favor.

It was Gouger's financial accounts that implicated the missionaries, for when they were examined by the Burmese it was found that he had paid sums of money at various times to Adoniram and Price. They failed to understand that Gouger was only cashing their checks, which he later sent to his own Calcutta bank for reimbursement. The Burmese could not envisage anybody being so stupid as to give away good silver ticals in exchange for "useless" pieces of paper. It was perfectly clear; the American missionaries were spies in the pay of the English.

On the afternoon of June 8, 1824, the Judsons were about to sit down for dinner when they heard a terrible commotion outside. Suddenly the door of their house was broken open and in rushed more than a dozen Burmese led by two fearsome-looking characters—one flourishing a black book and the other bearing the dreaded tattooed spot on either cheek. Ann gripped the table, for she had seen Spotted Faces, as they were called, before. Everyone knew how these "children of the prison" were cut off from all contact with law-abiding citizens, so that they were forced even to marry others of their kind. When their own prison terms were completed, they were appointed executioners, torturers and jailers. Sometimes the Burmese equivalent of the words *Murderer* or *Thief* was branded on their foreheads or breasts, while others might have lost either an ear or an eye.

The man carrying the black book shouted in a loud voice, "Where is the teacher?"

Ann's heart was thumping like a sledge hammer as her husband stepped forward. Koo-chil the cook stood shaking, with a large dish of rice in his hands.

"Here," replied Adoniram trying to remain calm.

199

"You are called by the King," said the man with the black book.

This was all the other Spotted Face was waiting to hear. Springing at Adoniram, he threw him to the ground, where with a jujitsulike movement born of long practice he leapt on his back and slipped a cord around his arms above the elbow. Then he pulled the cord tight, making Adoniram flinch with pain. This was too much for Ann, who flung herself upon the Spotted Face and had to be forcibly torn away. "Stay!" she screamed. "I will give you money."

The Spotted Face was furious that a woman should have dared to attack him in the course of his duties; so was the other pompous official with the black book.

"Arrest her too," stormed the latter. "She also is a foreigner." A moment later, however, realizing he might be overstepping his authority, he rescinded the order.

Adoniram was dragged from the house protesting his innocence and leaving the mission in a turmoil. The little girls Abby and Mary Hasseltine were screaming, and the masons building the new brick house had disappeared, while the servants were shivering with fright.

Ann gave a handful of silver to Maung Ing, the fisherman, telling him to follow Adoniram and try to bribe the Spotted Face to loosen the cord for she knew how a victim's arms could be jerked out of joint from such treatment.

It was some time before Maung Ing returned, his sorrowful face telling the worst before he spoke. Bruised and bleeding, Adoniram had been dragged through the streets to the prison called Let-may-yoon which in English meant *Hand Shrink Not*. A more applicable title would have been the Prison of Death.

200

Ann had little time for tears. She had hardly calmed herself when a magistrate stamped up onto the verandah, ordering her outside into the compound for interrogation. Barricaded in her bedroom she made him wait while she destroyed correspondence with sympathetic friends she had met in England, together with much of her diary containing descriptions of Burmese life. She believed these might be interpreted as further evidence of spying for the British. Finally she appeared before the magistrate, who was very upset at being kept waiting. She was a match for all his questions. At last, still in a rage, he departed leaving "a guard of ten ruffians" to watch her.

Night descended over the city. She had never known such

darkness; not a sound could be heard from any of the neighbors. Ann barred her front door, which infuriated the guards.

"Unbar the doors and come out or we will break the house down," shouted the chief guard. Ann retaliated as loudly, declaring that in the morning she would report them to the magistrate for threatening her. The guards whispered among themselves, and then through the window opening she saw the legs of her two Bengali servants being forced into some hastily constructed bamboo stocks.

Ann called for the chief guard. "Release them and in the morning I will make you all a present," she promised.

The chief guard grinned, the servants were released and Ann, cradling the weeping Abby and Mary in her arms, fell into a restless sleep.

Morning came at last, and Maung Ing managed to slip out of the prison gates for news of Adoniram. With him he took some food. He returned with the news that the teacher was still alive although his legs were held fast by three pairs of fetters locked to a long pole. Ann was terrified. When the magistrate again arrived to question her, she begged permission to go in person to some of the high government officials and plead for her husband. The magistrate, still provoked by her behavior of the day before, refused. "You might escape," he explained.

Then she remembered the King's own sister, the wife of Prince M.; in happier times she had been friendly with Adoniram. Ann asked if she might send the princess a letter begging for help. The magistrate agreed, but the letter came back with the excuse that Prince M.'s wife "did not understand it." Actually she was afraid to approach her regal brother because of the Queen, whose supposed powers of witchcraft she feared.

The day dragged by slowly giving Ann time to think more

clearly. The guards were still in her compound; once more she dreaded nightfall. Finally common sense recommended that if she were pleasant to them they might show respect. With her own hands she gave them green tea, ginger, rice and cigars. In return they allowed her to sleep once more with the children inside the mission house. Next morning, feeling somewhat refreshed, Ann decided on a simple plan. She could not think why it had not occurred to her before, for no Burmese could ever refuse a present! Off went a note to the governor saying that she wished to call upon him with a gift. The trick worked, for in no time she was allowed to leave the compound.

The governor was not unfriendly. After presenting what she had brought she complained bitterly that the white foreigners were being badly treated in the *Hand Shrink Not*. Besides, Dr. Jonathan Price and her own husband were not even English; they were American teachers!

"It is not in my power to release them from the prison, or from their irons," said the governor. "There is my head officer. You must consult with him as to how this is to be done." He pointed to a scowling man nearby to whose unfortunate face Ann took an instant dislike, later declaring it "presented the most perfect assemblage for all the evil passions attached to human nature."

Once outside the governor's house, the ugly man informed her that not only were the prisoners at his mercy, but she was also. Their future treatment depended solely upon her generosity.

Ann was not surprised, for she prided herself on being a good judge of character. Promptly she inquired the price.

"Pay me two hundred ticals, two pieces of fine cloth and two pieces of handkerchiefs."

Thoughtfully she had brought some money with her, but of course had no cloth. However, the sight of the money

203

was enough for the officer, who greedily accepted it. Minutes passed before, armed with the city governor's own order inscribed on a palm leaf, she was hurrying in the direction of her husband's prison. Trembling, she handed the permit to the guards at the gate and they let her inside. Then Adoniram was sent for. Slowly, on hands and knees, his torn clothing alive with vermin, he crawled painfully toward her. She opened her mouth with horror but no words came. To the day she died Ann Hasseltine Judson never forgot that terrible moment. Was this the glory of personal martyrdom which, years before in America, they had both envisaged? Now that it had actually arrived Ann did not think she would be strong enough to bear the cross.

She pulled herself together. Hiding her face was not going to help matters. Practically, Adoniram suggested more gifts of money in the right places as holding the most hope of release. Suddenly a group of Spotted Faces decided the visit had gone on long enough. "Get out or we will pull you out," they mocked her. She tried to argue, but to no avail; so, turning for a last look at the bedraggled figure in fetters, she passed sadly through the gates.

Ann Judson did not then know how successful she had really been through her attempt to seek help from the wife of Prince M. and the governor. All the foreigners were moved from the dreadful main prison building to an open shed in the walled compound where at least there was fresh air to breathe. How grateful the others were when it was discovered that Adoniram's wife had been responsible.

Even after the visit Ann did not know all the intimate details of the dreaded *Hand Shrink Not* Prison. The prison had no windows, so that the heat and stench were overpowering. On arrival Adoniram had been greeted at the gates by the prison governor upon whose naked breast was branded the dread word LOO-THAT (murderer). Affectionately he called Adoniram his own *beloved child,* then with a smile said that in return he liked to be known as *Father.*

After the introduction to his new 'parent' Adoniram was dragged off to a granite block where three stout pairs of fetters were awaiting his ankles. Father rubbed his hands together. "Now, walk, my child." he ordered. Adoniram tried, only to fall in the dust, from which uncomfortable position two Spotted Faces promptly dragged him inside the main prison, where another of their number armed with a club threw him into a corner.

Looking around he saw that the floor was covered with the half-naked forms of several dozen other prisoners, a few of whom were women. Some were lying confined in a multiple set of stocks made from great logs placed on top of one another, while from the ceiling by means of pulleys dangled a horizontal pole. Adoniram was soon to know its sinister use.

Gouger, Rodgers and Laird were already among Father's unfortunate children. Price was not long in joining them.

At nightfall an earthen lamp filled with crude oil was lit. Then the bamboo pole was lowered from above, pushed through the fettered legs of those prisoners not already in the stocks and again drawn upwards. Only the heads and shoulders of Father's children were resting on the muck-strewn floor. In this agonizing position they heard him bid them a pleasant "Good night."

Back at the tiny mission house Ann decided on her next course of action. The Burmese might believe their queen a witch, but after all back in New England Ann had been brought up on tales of witches. If the Queen held such power over her husband, then she was the logical person to petition for Adoniram's release. Ann had a slight acquaintance with the wife of the Queen's brother. Surely she could get such a petition to her sister-in-law.

Dressed in her beloved Burmese costume augmented by black laced ankle boots, Ann called upon the Queen's sister-in-law whom she described disapprovingly as "lolling on her carpet." Of course she had not forgotten to bring a present (it was fortunate she had thought to bring a good supply on returning from America). While the princess was opening it Ann told her how Adoniram and Dr. Price were being unfairly imprisoned, and in addition they were not English.

"Your case is not singular," said the princess, putting her gift aside and helping herself to a piece of pickled ginger.

"But it *is* singular. The teachers are Americans," insisted Ann. "They are ministers of religion and have nothing to do with war or politics, and they came to Ava in obedience to the King's command. They have never done anything to deserve such treatment. Is it right they should be treated thus?"

The princess thought carefully for a moment. "I am not the King," she said sympathetically. "What can I do?"

"You can state their case to the Queen and obtain their release," suggested Ann. "Place yourself in my situation: were you in America, and your husband, innocent of crime, thrown into prison, in irons—and you a solitary, unprotected female—what would you do?"

The princess fidgeted with the bracelets on her arms. "I will present your petition," she promised. "Come again tomorrow."

Ann's satisfaction at this minor success was short-lived,

for later that day she heard that Henry Gouger's possessions valued at fifty thousand dollars had been confiscated by the King. She was politely informed that her house was next on the list; it would be searched on the morrow.

Realizing that if everything of value were taken she would be unable to provide food or help for the imprisoned Adoniram, she gathered up most of the silver and small items of value, wrapped everything in a cloth, and, when it was dark, buried the bundle in the garden. The precious New Testament manuscript destined to form so vital a part of Adoniram's Burmese Bible was similarly wrapped and committed to a shallow grave in another part of the garden.

Next morning the Royal Treasurer arrived at the mission accompanied by other noblemen and an escort of fifty men, enough to strike terror into the heart of any lone woman. Ann decided that by keeping calm and showing good manners she might still defeat the main purpose of their visit. She kept thinking of the treasures buried in her garden!

She greeted the Royal Treasurer with as much courtesy as if she had been receiving guests in her parents' house at Bradford. Then she served green tea and sweetmeats. The officials were impressed. "At least," they thought, "she does not act like a guilty person."

"Where are your silver, gold and jewels?" inquired the Royal Treasurer, putting down his teacup.

Ann faced him innocently. "I have no gold or jewels, but here is the key of a trunk which contains the silver. Do with it as you please." She watched as the treasurer carefully weighed what was left of the silver, having thoughtfully brought along a scale for the purpose.

Casually she remarked, "This money was collected in America by the disciples of Christ, and sent here for the purpose of building a *kyoung,* and for our support while teaching the religion of Christ. Is it suitable that you should take it?"

This seemed to upset the Royal Treasurer, for the Burmese disapproved of stealing religious offerings. "We will state this circumstance to the King," promised another official. "Perhaps he will restore it."

"But is this all the silver you have?" asked the Treasurer.

Ann was caught, her Christian principles forbidding her to tell a lie. Faced by this predicament, she decided to play for time.

"The house is in your possession," was her answer. "Search for yourselves."

"Have you not deposited some silver with some person of your acquaintance?"

"My acquaintances are all in prison," Ann replied, forcing a little laugh. "With whom should I deposit silver?"

"Have you already given any silver to anyone in the government?"

Mrs. Judson was just waiting for such a question. Delighted, she confessed to having been forced to pay a two hundred tical bribe to no less a personage than the City Governor himself.

The house was then thoroughly searched, the trunks emptied and what was found to be "nice" or "curious" immediately confiscated, after which the officers began sorting the clothing.

"It would be disgraceful to take clothes partly worn into the presence of His Majesty, and to us they are of unspeakable value," sniffed Ann, her voice full of disgust. The clothes were left behind, although they were carefully listed, together with all Adoniram's books and medicines. She even dissuaded them from stealing Elnathan's work table and rocker. Then the inquisitors left.

As soon as they were out of sight Ann hurried back to the home of the Queen's brother, where his wife again received her. "I stated your case to the Queen," was her greeting, "but Her Majesty replied, 'The teachers will not die. Let them remain as they are.'" Ann thanked her for her trouble, then wearily walked towards the prison where she now realized Adoniram would have to remain.

However there was an encouraging aftermath to the Royal Treasurer's visit, for she was told it had been reported to the Golden Ears that "Yoodthan is a true teacher. We found nothing in his house but what belongs to priests. In addition to this money there are an immense number of books, medicines, trunks of wearing apparel, and like things, of which we have only taken a list. Shall we take them, or let them remain?"

"Let them remain," the Golden Lips replied, "and put this property [the silver] by itself, for it shall be restored to him again if he is found innocent."

Day after day without success Ann pestered the prison jailers to allow her to see Adoniram. Once she did manage to bribe one of them but the unfortunate fellow was caught, beaten and placed in the stocks. Feeling herself to be responsible for his uncomfortable predicament Ann sent for Father who graciously accepted twenty ticals to release him.

Ann was responsible for Adoniram's meals and Gouger was fed by a faithful servant, while most of the other prisoners were supplied with food by generous Burmese as acts of virtue. During the big religious festivals baskets of rice and ngapi were carried into the *Hand Shrink Not Prison*. The King was even supposed to have decreed that a basket of rice be given each prisoner although it never reached them.

After a while Adoniram was allowed to receive his food at the gate, where Ann thought of various ways of smuggling him messages. First she wrote notes on a biscuitlike cake which was baked hard and then placed in his dish of rice. In return he sent messages that became visible only when the tiles on which they were written were dipped in water. Their most successful method of communication was simply hiding a note in the teapot spout.

Later Ann was to write a little of her feelings to Elnathan, Adoniram's brother:

O, how many, many times have I returned from that dreary prison at nine o'clock at night, solitary, and worn out with fatigue and anxiety, and thrown myself down in that same rocking chair which you and Deacon L. provided for me in Boston, and endeavored to invent some new schemes for the release of the prisoners. Sometimes, for a moment or two, my thoughts would glance toward America, and my beloved friends there; but for nearly a year and a half, so entirely engrossed was every thought with present scenes and sufferings, that I seldom reflected on a single occurrence of my former life or recollected that I had a friend in existence out of Ava.

Not for one moment did she spare herself, for each slight possibility of her husband's release had to be explored. Everything humanly possible Ann did to ease his sufferings.

She supplied him with clean clothes, including his trousers, for as she told Father, with her New England upbringing it seemed to her that a gentleman whether he be in prison or not would be no gentleman without them.

The jailers, intrigued with the strange foreign woman who nevertheless herself preferred to wear Burmese clothing, carried out her wishes. Half amused, they handed Adoniram his Bengalese tailor-made trousers "cut in the best English fashion."

Meanwhile there were some officials who refused to leave her in peace. Once she was actually accused of having given a string of pearls, a pair of diamond earrings and a silver teapot to a Burmese officer. Arraigned at the courthouse, in the presence of hundreds of people she was ordered to "speak the truth or die."

"It is not true. If you, or any other person, can produce these articles I refuse not to die," was her quiet answer to the charge. Nobody could, so she was released. Before leaving the court she could not resist the opportunity that such an audience offered to plead for the release of her beloved Adoniram.

Every day she visited the Queen's sister-in-law; often Burmese friends gave her food for her husband. Bribes had to be found to pay the Spotted Faces on certain days when they had decided the prisoners should go unfed.

The City Governor was very upset with Ann for having revealed her "gift" to him of two hundred ticals.

"You are very bad. Why did you tell the Royal Treasurer that you had given me so much money?" His voice could be heard out in the street.

"The Treasurer inquired," replied Ann. "What could I say?"

"Say that you had given nothing, and I would have made the prisoners comfortable. Now I know not what will be their fate."

"But I cannot tell a falsehood," she explained. "My religion differs from yours. It forbids lying. If you had stood by me with your knife raised, I could not have said what you want."

All this time his wife, who was very outspoken and liked

211

to dominate him, had been listening. Ann's manner took her fancy. "Very true," she declared with a toss of her head. "What else could she have done? I like such straightforward conduct. You must not be angry with her." The City Governor, who always obeyed his wife, sat down on a cushion. He accepted the fine opera glass from England which Ann had brought for his present.

"I will try to make you presents which will make up for your loss," she maneuvered.

"You may intercede for your husband only," he told her. "For *your sake* he may remain where he is. But let the other prisoners take care of themselves."

Adoniram was allowed to stay in the open shed while the other foreign prisoners were again put in the terrible stinking main cell. Price was finally permitted to rejoin Adoniram after Ann had promised Father two handkerchiefs and some broadcloth as an inducement. Father had been persuaded by the foreign prisoners to give them some scissors to crop their hair short. In this way their heads were not so attractive to vermin.

Henry Gouger was by far the most cheerful of the prisoners. The sixteen-year-old daughter of one of the Spotted Faces had fallen in love with him. She even gave him water for washing, while to show his affection he would spear fat, juicy rats to fry for her father's supper.

One day Adoniram himself received a favorite dish— Ann's first Burmese mince pie, concocted from a mixture of water buffalo meat and plantains. The sight of this simple reminder of his boyhood days in New England was too much. He burst into tears.

Ann had a further surprise. They were going to have another baby. As far as she could tell, it would arrive in January or February.

212

twenty-one

Ann cultivated her friendship with the City Governor
and his domineering wife. In turn the Governor became so
fond of Mrs. Yoodthan that he judged her worthy of a
Burmese name. He called her Tsa-yar-ga-dau—*Eminent
Wife of the Big Teacher.*

Tsa-yar-ga-dau was now allowed to build her husband
a small private shed in the prison compound. She carried
earthenware pots of water inside for his toilet. How the
cleanliness-loving Adoniram loved her that day.

His major worry was the manuscript of the New Testament. Left buried in the garden it would soon rot, yet where
could they hide it in safety? He suggested to Ann, who was
now allowed to visit him privately in the little shed, that

she sew it inside a pillow so hard that no Spotted Face would trouble to steal it. Ann did as she was told, and the next night Adoniram was actually sleeping on the hard, ragged pillow containing his most precious possession.

Meanwhile the war with the British continued, and day after day the prisoners eagerly waited for news. The King had decreed that a cannon was to be fired twice over the river to announce a Burmese victory, once for a British victory and three times if the invaders had been driven from the land. So far the cannon had been fired only once.

An Irish soldier named Cassiday, captured while hunting pineapples for his breakfast, was added to the prisoners' number. Arriving with a large chain round his waist, he was immediately staked like a dog to a post in the floor. Cassiday, a private serving with the East India Company's Madras European regiment, had firsthand stories to tell of the fighting. Questioned by the Wungyis, he shook their morale when he told them, "I think we should make short work of your army, if they are no better than those we met in the stockades. My regiment has great experience with the bayonet."

By this time the Wungyis knew enough about the bayonet to realize he was telling the truth, for the invaders had stormed the Burmese stockades at Rangoon and captured them. The Burmese were even inclined to believe the story that after a battle the wounded British recovered their lost arms and legs for the surgeons to sew back in place again.

The Golden Presence decided that only Bandula could successfully beat the British, but he had already been dispatched through a pass in the mountains to attack them via Arakan which adjoined British-controlled territory. When the British had made their surprise sea attack on Rangoon, with craft which included the first steamboat ever seen by the Burmese, the city had been almost undefended. Bandula's great army was successful in vanquishing small outposts in the vicinity of Arakan, and the King mistook these minor triumphs for great victories. In triumph Bandula was recalled, while, much against their will, fresh soldiers were conscripted at one hundred ticals apiece. The Burmese forces near Rangoon had already suffered two crushing defeats, but the royal advisers in Ava were loath to admit their previous appraisal of the British invaders might be wrong.

Gouger and Adoniram continued their friendship in prison, where they improvised a crude chess set, spending many hours in this occupation. They were even used by now to the dread hour of three in the afternoon, which was execution time. Every day somebody was carried outside to die.

Dr. Price was Adoniram's biggest personal anxiety, for he never knew what his fellow missionary was going to do next. Once Price told Father he could make him a clock from a lump of clay. Of course he failed, poor Father having to be content with the model of a head showing the compartments of the human brain, more suitable for a doctor's surgery than a jail. He even removed a growth attached to a Spotted Face's eyelid. Adoniram prayed that the fellow would not die, making them all the subject of possible reprisals. The operation was partially successful, the man's sight being unimpaired, although he could no longer open his eyelid in a natural manner. Instead, it had to be opened and shut with his finger, like a curtain. Even this did not unnecessarily alarm Price, who insisted, "The eye will keep all the better. When you want it, all you have to do is lift the lid with your finger; and when you have done with it, let it drop again." Surprisingly the Spotted patient was satisfied.

At night the prisoners had to sleep close together, and it was at this time that Jonathan Price most annoyed Adoniram. Adoniram had been studying the doctrine of "quietism" as perfected by Madame Guyon, a French Roman Catholic, and Price seemed to do nothing but spoil his efforts. Price liked to sleep with his knees in a position almost level with his nose, and often his fettered legs would unconsciously lunge outwards, pounding Adoniram in the back. After three such blows in one night Adoniram lost his temper, shouting, "Brother Price, you are a public nuisance! I insist on your sleeping as other people do."

The more Price argued that his bad dreams were the cause, the more upset Adoniram became. At last he offered to fight the doctor, but Gouger gallantly intervened, promising to sleep between them. Secretly, the Englishman was amused at the prospect of two missionaries engaging in a fist-fight.

With Gouger in the middle Adoniram was able to lull himself to sleep with Madame Guyon's helpful verse which William Cowper the English poet had translated.

> *No bliss I seek, but to fulfill,*
> *In life and death, Thy lovely will;*
> *No succor in my woes I want,*
> *Except what Thou art pleased to grant.*

In spite of her pregnancy Ann continued to work on behalf of her husband and the other foreign prisoners. In September Bandula was back in the capital, more powerful than ever, with the conduct of the war entirely in his hands. Ann decided that if she could plead personally before him something might still be done, for he seemed to command more authority now than the King himself.

It was a risky undertaking, for—as several friendly courtiers told her—if Bandula was reminded that the white men were still alive he might be tempted to order their immediate execution. She consulted Adoniram, who thought they might just as well be hung for sheep as lambs and wrote the petition for the release of the American teachers himself. Mustering her courage, Ann carried it into Bandula's awesome presence.

He was curious at the sudden appearance of the foreign woman and listened courteously as a secretary read him Adoniram's message. Ann readily answered the questions he had to ask about their work and reason for being in Burma. He was not unpleasant, telling her to call again and after he had thought more on the subject he would give her an answer.

Delighted over her success with Bandula, Ann hurried to the prison so as not to keep Adoniram in suspense longer than necessary. He was much pleased, thinking that now there might be some real chance of release; but Ann's friend the City Governor was not so encouraging, believing that her rashness might result in all the foreign prisoners' being put to death.

When Ann paid her return visit to Bandula she took care to take the most expensive present left among her dwindling supply. His wife received her with the disappointing message that "He [Bandula] was now very busily employed in making preparations for Rangoon, but when he had retaken that place and expelled the British, he would return and release all the prisoners."

Thoroughly disheartened, Ann walked slowly home, sure

now that only the ending of the war would spell release for her husband. This did not mean any lessening of her efforts to make Adoniram as comfortable as possible while in prison. Nearly every day she visited the home of the City Governor, whose dominating wife was still very fond of her. For hours she would tell them both about life in America, of which they could never hear enough. They found it hard to believe she had come from a land that in winter turned white with something called snow. In return for her time spent amusing the Governor with such stories she was given a permit to visit the prison each day. The Spotted Faces, by this time rather impressed by the foreign woman's intense loyalty to her husband, would usually let her in.

By November, Bandula with an army of sixty thousand had reached the outskirts of Rangoon. He had boasted to the Prince of Sarawady that "In eight days I shall dine in the public hall at Rangoon and afterwards return thanks in the Shwe-Dagon pagoda." By sheer force of numbers this did seem possible, but the well-trained British forces, comprising thirteen hundred Europeans and twenty-five hundred Sepoys, were waiting to receive them. Twenty guns were pointed from the main platform of the towering pagoda; there were gunboats lying at all the strategic positions in the river and neighboring creeks.

On December 1, 1824, Bandula picked out the Shwe-Dagon pagoda for his main attack, which was completely defeated, for muskets, spears and swords were no match for the up-to-date British guns. He retreated with the shattered remnants of his army, and the British themselves were too tired to follow. For some reason he encamped only a short distance from the city where he was again attacked a few days later. Once more the Burmese were

218

scattered, Bandula escaping with only seven thousand of his former army of sixty thousand men.

When the dread news reached Ava there was great consternation, especially among the women. Suddenly Ann found herself very popular among the royal ladies at court, for everybody now wanted her advice. What with regular visits to Adoniram and the City Governor plus "requests" to call on the Queen Mother and various princesses, Ann, far advanced in her pregnancy, found the days far too short. The Queen Mother and the Princesses of Shwedong and Pugan begged her counsel, for they had heard that the invading foreigners would eat them alive. "The Bandula's troops have piled up their arms for the use of the foreigners. They have all dispersed, and the enemy has nothing to do but march to Ava, clapping his hands."

The Royal ladies implored Ann to tell them what to do. Would they really be safe if they stayed? Would she help protect them? Ann reassured them as best she could, saying that the British were very fond of royalty. Meantime she promised to help them if they would do the same for Adoniram and the other foreign prisoners.

On January 26, 1825, Ann gave birth to her baby. It was a girl, the tiniest, saddest thing she had ever set eyes upon. All her worries, hardships and privations had left their mark on this child, so different in appearance from the beautiful, healthy-looking little boy they had lost.

Tiny or not, Ann gave the baby a very long name. It was Maria Elizabeth Butterworth. For twenty days she did not feel strong enough to walk to the prison. When at last she managed to do so Adoniram hobbled to the gate to see his new daughter. Even the Spotted Faces assembled to look at the child. They could not have been more excited if they had all been its father, for so white a baby they had

219

never set on eyes on. Gouger speared them some appetizing rats and they all went off to celebrate.

Adoniram promptly sat down to compose twenty-four verses in honor of Maria Elizabeth Butterworth Judson, dedicating them to an "Infant Daughter, twenty days old, in the condemned prison at Ava."

> Sleep, darling infant, sleep,
> Hushed on thy mother's breast;
> Let no rude sound of clanking chains
> Disturb thy balmy rest. . .

The war continued to go against the Burmese. The Pakan Wun, Bandula's second-in-command, was thrown into the Let-may-yoon on a charge of treason. The Spotted Faces were delighted to see him. So important a man could only mean large bribes for themselves.

March came, and with it the most terrifying day Adoniram and his companions had known since they had first entered the dread prison. They were fitted with two extra pairs of fetters and the Spotted Faces talked in whispers while they tore down Ann's bamboo hut. Adoniram's heart turned sick when the precious pillow containing his translation of the New Testament was snatched up and carried away. The Spotted Faces seemed determined to hide all evidence that the foreign prisoners had ever been incarcerated in their jail. There was the dreadful sound of the sharpening of knives against stone. The other prisoners were whispering amongst themselves. Surely it could only mean that at last the foreigners were to be executed.

Ann received her first information that something was amiss when news was brought her by the faithful Maung Ing that Adoniram was back inside the main prison with two extra sets of fetters. A Spotted Face who admired her integrity had told him. Also, Maung Ing said, the little hut she had built was gone and the pillows belonging to the white prisoners had been confiscated.

At once Ann rushed over to the City Governor. He was out, but anticipating her visit, he had left a message with his wife that Ann must on no account "ask to have the additional fetters taken off, or the prisoners released, for *it could not be done.*"

Ann's mind was in a turmoil at this news. Across the street not a living soul could be seen in the prison, not even the Spotted Faces.

Hurrying back to her house two miles away, Ann fed Maria and then returned, hoping that this time her friend the City Governor might be back. She was fortunate: he was.

He was really embarrassed. He pretended to show anger, yet the shame in his heart seeped through. Protocol compelled him to listen to her pleading and every sentence she spoke jabbed like a spear at his heart.

"Your Lordship has hitherto treated us with the kindness of a father. Our obligations to you are very great. We have looked to you for protection from oppression and cruelty. You have often eased the sufferings of the unfortunate innocents in your charge. You promised me especially that you would stand by me to the last, and even though you should receive an order from the King, you would not put Mr. Judson to death. What crime has he committed to deserve such additional punishment?"

She bowed her head; the Governor's wife turned slowly and walked out of the room, while her husband actually began to cry. Ann had never seen a Burmese official show such emotion before; the sight was strangely moving.

"I pity you, Tsa-yar-ga-dau*," he said, his voice shaking. "I knew how you would make me feel. Therefore I forbade your application. You must believe me when I say that I do not want to increase the sufferings of the prisoners. When I am ordered to execute them, the least I can do is to put them out of sight. I will now tell you what I have never told you before, that three times I have received suggestions from the Queen's brother to assassinate all the white prisoners privately. But I would not do it. And now I repeat it: though I execute all the others, I will never execute your husband. But I cannot release him from his present confinement, and you must not ask it.

* Tsa-yar-ga-dau: Ann's spelling. Probably Sa-ya (gyi) ga-dau meaning *Eminent Wife of the Big Teacher.*

twenty-two

"Bandula has won a victory!" The sound of the two guns booming over the river filled the disheartened residents of Ava with delight. His name was on every lip although actually he had only beaten off an attack on his entrenchments. Poor Bandula's glory was short-lived, for on April 1 he was blown to pieces by a shell.

Arriving in Ava from the front, Bandula's brother was promptly beheaded. Panic filled the streets. Even the sorceress queen beat upon her breast moaning, "*Ama! Ama!* (Alas! Alas!)"

The crafty Pakan Wun saw in Bandula's death a chance for his own release. Promptly he sent word to the Golden Ears that he had an excellent plan for defeating the British.

Instantly he was freed, the Golden Presence receiving him at the palace in spite of the rule that none who on the King's orders had worn fetters should again pass through the palace gates. The Pakan Wun was given full powers necessary for winning the war. He promised to pay the sum of a hundred ticals in advance to every volunteer soldier, predicting that this time the British would really be driven into the sea.

Lanciego the Spaniard, tax collector at Rangoon and the only foreigner not in prison, was arrested on the charge that he had sold the island of Negrais to the British. Even under torture he refused to admit his guilt.

Adoniram fell sick with a fever in the inner prison, probably caused by the intense heat coupled with the dreadful smells. Ann would not have known this but for the notes hidden in the teapot spout. One of these was found, with the result that she herself was almost arrested. Each day food still had to be taken to the prison gates to feed him. Sometimes several times in one day the City Governor patiently received her pleas for help. Next to his own wife he had never known such a persistent woman. *Would she never give up?*

Finally, sick and tired of his Tsa-yar-ga-dau's pleadings, the City Governor capitulated, writing her the necessary permit on a palm leaf. Father seemed pleased to see Yood-than's wife again, even asking after the white baby. He let her build a fresh hut in the yard for her husband where she could treat him with medicines. He also returned Adoniram's hard pillow, not suspecting its contents. After seeing her sick husband safely into his new surroundings, Ann commented that it was a "palace in comparison with the place he had just left."

On May 2, 1825, while ministering to Adoniram in the

224

little hut, she was suddenly ordered to go to the Governor's house. She was immediately suspicious, because nothing like this had ever happened before. Adoniram was worried too. He made her promise to return and tell him what the Governor wanted.

On confronting the Governor, she found he merely wanted to question her about the inside of a European pocket watch. More relieved than angry that he had interrupted her precious meeting with Adoniram, she was obliged to stay some time and talk with him. At last he was ready to let her go, his face wearing a big smile. Quickly she crossed the road to the prison gates but even before she reached them one of her servants intercepted her, shouting, "The white prisoners have been taken away."

Rushing back to the Governor, she demanded to know if it were true. He had to admit that it was. His object in sending for her had been only to spare her the pain of parting from Adoniram.

Where had they taken him? She ran through the streets, inquiring if anybody had seen in which direction the foreign prisoners were taken. At last she met an old woman who told her they had gone in the direction of the Mootangai, a tributary of the Irrawaddy. Her lungs half bursting, she ran towards the river, but there was no sign of those she sought. Back she went to the City Governor.

"The prisoners are to be sent to Amarapura," he told her, just having received the information. "Why, I know not. I will send off a man immediately to see what is to be done with them." Then he looked once more on Tsa-yar-ga-dau. "Take care of yourself," he begged.

At nightfall the kindly Governor procured a cart for Ann, as he had been against her venturing into the streets alone. Returning to the mission house, she quickly packed her trunks and medicine chest. These she had lifted into the cart to take back to the City Governor for safekeeping, for she was determined to go in search of Adoniram. Later Henry Gouger's faithful servant was able to give her the reassuring news that her husband with the other prisoners was in Amarapura. They were to be taken on the morrow to another village, the name of which he did not know.

Next morning Ann set out by river for Amarapura. It was a scorchingly hot day. Even on the water there seemed to be no breeze at all. She was accompanied by the little Burmese girls Mary and Abby Hasseltine, Koo-chil her Bengalese cook and the little three-months-old baby Maria. The boat put them off a good two miles from the government house at Amarapura and it took much bargaining before a cart could be hired to take them there.

Ann had made many journeys since her marriage to Adoniram Judson but none more uncomfortable than the one to Amarapura. There was no relief from the sun and the cart had solid wooden wheels. By the time they arrived Ann was shaken and bruised all over, while the three children were vomiting and crying.

In Amarapura the City Governor was not unhelpful, finding her a guide. Off again they rumbled in the horrible bone-shaking cart to the village of Oung-pen-la where she had heard Adoniram was imprisoned. They arrived just before nightfall.

Ann had never seen such a jail! It was almost tumbling down. A number of Burmese were on top of the roof trying to patch it with palm leaves. Adoniram, exhausted from his own fearsome journey, was chained to one of the other prisoners. Still feverish and bordering on delirium, he gave one look at Ann and sobbed, "Why have you come? I hoped you would not follow. You cannot live here." Then he collapsed.

From the other prisoners she managed gradually to piece together details of the death march. The men, their fetters removed, had been roped together in pairs. A Spotted Face conveniently armed with a spear to goad them on was in charge of each two men, driving them forward like horses. For Adoniram, stripped of his shoes (unlike the other prisoners he had insisted on wearing them in prison), every step was sheer agony. The sun-scorched road strewn with rocks quickly blistered and lacerated his tender feet. Half dead from fever, parched for lack of water and in agony at every step, Adoniram, man of God though he was, on crossing the bridge over the Mootangai River was tempted to jump over.

"Gouger," he whispered, "the parapet is low. There can be no sin in our availing ourselves of this opportunity." Gouger prevailed against his doing so.

Ann's immediate task was to find food and a place to stay the night. Koh-bai the chief jailer refused to allow her to erect a bamboo shelter near the prison, saying, "It is not customary." There was no food to be had either. Seeing her distress, the man suddenly had a change of heart and gave her the use of a room in his own house. More of a store place than anything else, it was already half full of grain. Koo-chil lit a fire and boiled some water. There was nothing else. Hungry and tired, the children cried themselves to sleep.

Adoniram was mercifully in a state of stupor. His legs, along with those of his fellows, were put in the stocks, the bamboo pole again being raised by a pulley. The mosquitoes

227

flew in from the rice fields. The prisoners, their feet already bruised and bleeding, were in such excruciating pain that even their guards were moved to mercy, lowering the bamboo pole to enable the men to protect their bleeding feet.

Morning came and with it food, for a friend of Dr. Price in Amarapura arrived with rice and curry which Ann and the children shared with the prisoners at the invitation of the jailer. Henry Gouger hobbled out onto the prison verandah, where the fresh air smelt like heaven after the stench of their prison in Ava. The other prisoners, still unable to walk because of their sore feet, were unable to join him. Underneath the tumbledown prison were piled heaps of firewood, causing the prisoners to wonder if they were to be burned alive. They later discovered that the wood had only been placed there to reinforce the rotting floor.

Ann was allowed to visit her husband and found him a little better, although he could not get to his feet. In due course Gouger's baker turned up with salt fish and biscuits. Ann managed to buy some rice. Her most pressing anxiety was Mary, whose face was covered with spots.

Eventually Ann came to the dread realization that the child had smallpox. There seemed no course to take but to vaccinate the baby Maria and Abby. Ann herself had been vaccinated in America and had some idea of what to do. She had been told that inoculation from an infected person acted as a preventative on another. With the interested jailer's wife watching, she inoculated Maria and Abby with an ordinary needle. The jailer's wife then decided to have her own children done also. Maria's vaccination was not successful. The baby caught the smallpox, but Abby and the jailer's children were hardly affected. Ann's fame swept through the village. Soon she was being asked to inoculate

228

almost every child in the place. Fortunately for her none of them died.

While Ann was thus attending to the cares of the village, the prisoners' lot improved. The roof was repaired; fresh air brought color to the men's pale cheeks. Then one day another prisoner arrived—*a lioness*. Nobody seemed to know what she was doing there, least of all the jailer. Gingerly the cage was pulled inside the stockade on his orders. Adoniram was sure they were all to be eaten alive, although another prisoner considered the animal was there only as a symbol of England. No orders had come to feed the lioness, so the jailer did not trouble to do so. Its pitiful cries for food continued day and night. When at last it was given a pariah dog to eat, the poor creature was too far gone, dying shortly afterwards.

Adoniram kept looking at the empty lion cage. What a blessed retreat it would make, he thought. The jailor had no objection, so the missionary was moved into his new quarters. Ann compared him to Daniel in the lions' den, but the privacy so gained more than compensated for the teasing.

Maria and Mary were just recovering from smallpox when Ann began to suffer with a bad attack of dysentery. Half dead, she journeyed by cart back to Ava leaving Koo-chil the cook to look after the children.

Recovering the medicine chest from the City Governor, she dosed herself every few hours with laudanum. By sheer determination she managed to live through the grueling journey back to Oung-pen-la. Even Koo-chil broke down and sobbed when he saw his mistress, for he thought she was dying. Completely forgetting his caste, the Bengalese servant cared for Ann, who was totally unable to do anything for herself. He also looked after the children, searched for food and fed Adoniram.

Poor loyal Koo-chil; the only thing he could not do was to provide sustenance for the baby, for owing to Ann's sickness there was no supply of natural milk to feed Maria. Soon the baby's cries could be heard even in the prison, where they reached the ears of the helpless Adoniram. Koh-bai the jailer's wife, moved with compassion, persuaded her husband to allow Adoniram, still wearing his fetters, to hobble around the village with Maria in his arms begging a little milk from the nursing mothers. The sympathetic Burmese women were very obliging and little Maria lived. Later, of this time of sickness Ann wrote home to Bradford,

I now began to think the very afflictions of Job had come upon me. When in health I could bear the various trials and vicissitudes through which I was called to pass. But to be confined with sickness and unable to assist those who were dear to me, when in distress, was almost too much for me to bear, and had it not been for the consolations of religion, and an assured conviction that every additional trial was ordered by infinitive love and mercy, I must have sunk under my accumulated sufferings.

Never once, from the day Ann Hasseltine linked her destiny with that of Adoniram Judson, did she lose faith in her Christian convictions. Through every tribulation and hardship they rose up to succor her.

Ann slowly recovered her strength and life went on as before at Oung-pen-la. One day Gouger discovered that the Pakan Wun now in complete charge of the war against the British had been born in that very village. With horror he realized the significance of their presence in obscure Oung-pen-la. The Pakan Wun, so rumor said, planned to slaughter the foreigners in his own birthplace. Fortunately for them he died, a victim of his own importance, just three days before his intended arrival.

Gouger's baker brought the welcome news. The Pakan Wun who had asked the King to give him full command over that section of the armed forces controlled by the Shan princes, had requested the King's private bodyguard for his own protection and suggested to the Golden Lips that they should pray at the Mengoon Pagoda which, with its enormous bell, was located several miles from Ava. This was too much for King Bagyidaw. "Ha!" he stormed, "he would take away my guard and then have me leave my throne!" The very guard that the Pakan Wun had sought to acquire for himself then caught hold of his long hair and dragged him from the palace. He was hustled to the execution place outside the city walls where the royal elephants obligingly stamped him to death. The Golden Presence soon discovered a great deal of money in the late Pakan Wun's house which he was supposed to have used to encourage volunteers for the army.

The war was coming to an end. Sir Archibald Campbell, the British commander, had even offered the King of Burma a treaty but the Burmese were still suspicious. For one thing they had heard of the hundreds of British soldiers who had fallen victim to the cholera. The British might only be trying to save face because of their weakened numbers.

Adoniram and his fellow prisoners found themselves hustled into carts and taken to Amarapura. Here they were each placed in a separate room where each in turn was required to translate Sir Archibald's peace terms into Burmese. In this way, by comparing the individual efforts, the Burmese knew they could tell if the prisoners were translating the truth. Towards the end of October, 1825, Sir Archibald was informed by the Burmese that they had never heard of such a thing as relinquishing territories or paying indemnities. It was clear to him then that they were only trying to gain time.

November came, and on the fourth of the month Ann watched with joyful heart as Adoniram's fetters were removed. He was being released at last. Nobody at the Burmese army headquarters could write or speak English and the British were in a similar predicament; nobody at their camp could speak or write Burmese. Adoniram would make a wonderful translator.

There had been one completely unexpected difficulty about their leaving the village of Oung-pen-la. At the last minute the jailer had refused to let Ann accompany her husband, saying that the order to release Adoniram did not include her as well. "But I was not sent here as a prisoner. You have no authority over me," she protested, sensing it was the same old trick to get a present. She was right. After the customary gift-giving Mrs. Adoniram Judson had been allowed to leave for Amarapura with her husband, but Amarapura proved to be no haven, for they were immediately separated again. Adoniram was first taken before the Governor of the city and then to Ava. Ann was left to her own resources. Accompanied by Koo-chil, she went by boat to her own small house. Next morning her first call was on her old friend the City Governor. She knew he would explain Adoniram's position to her.

It seemed that for the time being her husband was still a prisoner but that this was only temporary. Eventually he would be sent to Maloun where the Burmese forces were encamped. There his services were needed as translator and advisor. The Governor had some good news to add concerning himself. He had just been promoted to a Wungyi. Tsa-yar-ga-dau thanked him, and congratulated him upon his own good fortune.

232

Next morning, November 7, 1825, the new Wungyi had thoughtfully arranged for Adoniram to call on Ann before leaving for Maloun. She quickly packed him food, mattress, blanket and pillow. All the other bedclothes had been looted while she had been at Oung-pen-la. She also had the most acceptable parting gift Adoniram Judson ever had in his life—*news that the precious translation of the New Testament was safe.*

Adoniram was overjoyed. It seemed that Maung Ing, his faithful convert, had gone to the Let-may-yoon Prison the day Adoniram had been transferred to Oung-pen-la, with the object of finding some little keepsake of his adored "Yoodthan." What he found was the middle of the pillow, which was in reality the translated manuscript hidden in some dirty, cottonlike material. Upon tearing away the rough pillowcase, the Spotted Face who confiscated it had decided the hard interior wasn't worth keeping and had promptly thrown it away.

Elated, Adoniram sailed for Maloun, three days' journey distant. He had been allowed one servant, a gift of twenty ticals (approximately ten dollars) from the government, and some half-spoiled rice. He was unable to stretch out full-length in the cramped quarters allotted to him. By the time he arrived, Adoniram was burning with fever and quickly became delirious.

Days passed before he was recovered enough to do the work for which he had been sent to Maloun. Finally his mind was clear enough to translate, and the Burmese seemed satisfied with his efforts. He tried hard to give them a few basic lessons in treaties and agreements as practiced by European nations, but the Burmese simply did not believe that warring peoples could be so honorable.

"Ah, that is noble! That is as it should be!" they would

say, "but the teacher dreams. He has a celestial spirit and he thinks himself in the land of celestial beings." To show their new-found appreciation of him they gave him a tiny cotton rug. At least part of his body would keep warm during the cold, damp nights.

Every day Burmese and British officials met for talks on board a vessel moored in the river. Among other things the British demanded a crore of rupees (approximately a million British pounds sterling), together with the territories of Arakan, Assam, Manipur and Tenasserim. The Burmese would be allowed fifteen days of armistice to take the treaty to the Golden Presence.

Suddenly, on December 17, Adoniram was returned to Ava. After fifteen days of hearing nothing from the Burmese, the British advanced on Maloun, where the only item of importance they found in the Burmese camp was their own peace treaty. Nobody had had the courage to lay it in the Golden Hands!

Poor Adoniram; he passed so close to his own home that he could actually see the lights in the windows, yet was not allowed to go in. Frustrated, he was locked in a shed attached to the courthouse at Ava. It seemed that he was to be returned to the prison at Oung-pen-la. Maung Ing discovered him after he had been there all day without food. The servant who had gone down-river to Maloun with Adoniram had furnished the information concerning his return.

Answering Adoniram's anxious inquiries concerning the welfare of Ann and their baby daughter, Maung Ing was somewhat evasive. He kept repeating that Mrs. Yoodthan wished him to appeal to the governor of the North Gate to see if Adoniram must return to Oung-pen-la. When he had gone Adoniram began to worry. Was Ann really all right?

The governor of the North Gate was more than sympathetic. He was extremely practical. Offering his own person as security, he applied next morning for Adoniram's release. It was the last day of the Western year. Adoniram thanked the governor with all his heart, and then he half walked, half ran to the mission house.

The flickering flame from the crude-oil lamp was still casting a feeble glow through the window when he reached his own home. Inside the door, warming herself over a brazier of coals, sat a Burmese woman nursing a thin and dirty baby. He did not even recognize it as his own little Maria and hurried into the bedroom where an awful sight confronted him. Stretched over the foot of the bed lay what looked to be the lifeless body of his wife. Her fine black curls had been cut from her head which was now covered with a grubby cotton cap; the chalk-white skin of her face stretched taut over her cheekbones. She looked more like a skeleton than a human being. Shocked, he gently lifted the forlorn figure into his arms and cradled it gently to his breast as one would a child. Even then he did not know if she were still alive. When her eyelids flickered he saw that she was.

Two weeks after he had left for Maloun Ann had fallen victim to cerebral meningitis, which the Burmese feared as the death-dealing spotted fever. When the first symptoms appeared Ann knew exactly what to expect, for in all probability the results would be fatal. A wet nurse arrived like a godsend at this crucial period to care for Maria's needs. After two weeks of this burning fever, during which time she had been unconscious, Dr. Price, released from prison to do translating, heard of Ann's plight and begged to see her. It was he who had ordered the shaving of her head and the application of hot blisters to both scalp and feet.

The Burmese women living close to the mission house

clustered sympathetically by the door while these operations were being performed. Shrugging her shoulders one of them said, "She is dead. If the king of angels should come in, he could not recover her." But the angels were not ready for Ann, and the crisis had been passed a month before Adoniram arrived to find her. As the days went by she became stronger. Because their house was located in a dangerous position by the river, they were forced early in 1826 to move farther into the city. A British attack was momentarily expected. The Golden City was in an uproar.

The North Gate Governor invited the Judsons to live with him. Adoniram and Price were now treated with great respect by the Burmese, who sought their advice every few hours. The Golden Ears had at last heard of the Treaty of Maloun; he even knew of the crore of rupees. Although the British had agreed, on payment of the indemnity, to leave all Burma with the exception of the coastal provinces to her own people, the King and his court simply could not believe they would keep their promise. Henry Gouger summed up the feelings of the Burmese exactly when he wrote, "Such an unheard-of thing as conquering a country and then restoring it was incredible! Measuring British faith and honor by their own standard, they concluded the intention was first to impoverish them, and then to march on the capital."

Two British officers, a Lieutenant Bennett and Dr. Sandford, had recently been taken prisoner, so the Burmese decided to make full use of them. Surely the British commander would agree to better terms. Adoniram was ordered to accompany Dr. Sandford to the British camp, but he was only too pleased to get out of this particular mission and let the eager Price take his place.

It was almost the end of January when Price and Sandford set sail down-river to contact the British. Meanwhile

Adoniram would be hostage for Price, and Bennett for Sandford.

Ava was the scene of frantic activity twenty-four hours a day as efforts were made to ensure its impregnability. Ann, describing the scene, wrote:

Men and beasts were at work night and day, making new stockades, and strengthening old ones, and whatever buildings were in their way were immediately torn down. Our house, with all that surrounded it, was levelled to the ground, and our beautiful little compound turned into a road and a place for the erection of cannon. All articles of value were conveyed out of town, and safely deposited in some other place.

Price and Sandford returned from the British camp with Sir Archibald's reply to the plea for better terms. The river banks were filled with silent, watching crowds as the boat carrying the two emissaries was rowed slowly into view. The Golden Eyes could not believe what they saw. Nobody had really thought for one minute that Price and Sandford would be fools enough to return to captivity when they might have remained in safety at the British camp. For the first time they realized that Adoniram might not be such a celestial being as they had supposed, and perhaps after all he had been telling them earthly truths. *As he had tried to tell them, the British might be crazy after all.*

While the King's advisers sat silently in the Hlut-dau, Price interpreted the British reply: "The general and commissioners will make no alteration in their terms, except that the indemnity may be paid at four different times. The first quarter must be paid within twelve days, or the army will continue their march. In addition, the prisoners in the hands of the Burmese must be given up immediately."

Then he told them that Sir Archibald had also demanded the release of all the other foreign prisoners. This was too much for the Golden Ears. The foreign prisoners he would gladly let go—they had been nothing but a nuisance—but the teacher Yoodthan, his remarkable wife and their child, he was unwilling to release; for at last he had come to realize how valuable the services of the Judsons might be.

"They are not English," he cried, "they are my people. They shall not go."

Adoniram put forth every effort to make the King's advisers see reason. He assured them that the British had to be paid before they would leave Burma, but still they were willing to wager their luck on one last chance. A general named Layar-thoo-yah suddenly decided he could yet beat the British. The ancient capital of Pagan could be fortified; he would stop them there.

The Golden Ears were pleased with what they heard. The general was given the title of "Lord of the Setting Sun" and his army of fifteen thousand men, all paid in advance a sum of a hundred and fifty ticals each, marched off to Pagan, on the way many buying rich clothing with their money. At the sight of nine hundred trained British soldiers they broke ranks and ran. The Lord of the Setting Sun was promptly executed.

The British army was getting closer; even the wicked Queen was frightened, ordering the King to raise the indemnity money. Priceless gold and silver ornaments were immediately melted down for the purpose. Even then the King's advisers hoped for a way out. It seemed terrible to surrender so much gold. Adoniram was sent to bargain with

Sir Archibald, who by this time had lost most of his patience. He replied that he would march slowly on Ava, giving the King one last chance to pay the first installment. Adoniram was to ask each foreigner in the threatened city if he wished to leave.

Adoniram returned with Sir Archibald's ultimatum. The unhappy chief Wungyi told each foreigner that he was free to go. To Adoniram he said, "You will not leave us; you will become a great man if you will remain."

The teacher shifted uneasily in his shoes. He did not particularly want to leave Burma. The war had nothing to do with him or his country. Had he not come to Burma to found a Christian mission? To offend the Burmese government in their time of need might well destroy the work he had already begun. He decided to be tactful, saying that his wife preferred at least for the time being to go. They would see that as her husband he was duty-bound to follow her. The Burmese agreed.

Late that night the piles of gold and silver bars were begrudgingly loaded into the waiting ships. Ann, emaciated and shaky from her terrible illness, was taken with the baby to join Adoniram on the riverbank. Even then the chief Wungyi requested them not to go, but Adoniram was adamant. The chief Wungyi shrugged his shoulders; Yoodthan might still be useful to them in the future. He did not want to upset him either.

For the last time Ann glanced back at the Golden City with its palaces and pagodas all newly ornamented and covered with gold. With Adoniram by her side she felt at peace as the golden boats from Burma slipped into the moonlit night.

ANN HASSELTINE JUDSON

After Adoniram's release by the Burmese late in 1825, his happiness was shortlived. On March 6, 1826, with Ann and the baby Maria he left Yandabo for Rangoon aboard the gunboat *Irrawaddy* only to find the mission house in a state of ruin. John Crawfurd, the newly appointed civil commissioner under Lord Amherst, British governor general, later persuaded Adoniram to travel to Ava as adviser and translator during the negotiation of a commercial treaty between the East India Company and the Burmese Government.

Ann and the baby were sent to Amherst, which the British had chosen to be capital of the provinces now under their control. Situated on a pleasant peninsula in the Sal-

241

ween River, it seemed to be the most likely place for Ann to regain her health. The British provided her with a temporary home where she immediately began to supervise the construction of a new mission house and school.

Unfortunately the hardships sustained at Oung-pen-la and Ava had permanently weakened her. On October 26, 1826, at the age of thirty-six, she died of fever contracted from the baby. Adoniram while still at Ava received the black-sealed letter containing the tragic news. Baby Maria joined her mother in death on April 24, 1827, aged two years and three months.

Following the Japanese occupation of Burma in World War II, Ann's grave and headstone were found undisturbed. Refusing money for the restoration of the monument and iron railing enclosure, a group of Burmese Christians insisted on doing the job themselves, using coconut fiber for the laborious task. Because of soil erosion, twice since Ann's burial in 1826—once quite recently—her body has lovingly been moved to new grave sites. The hopea (*hopea odorata*) tree that shaded the first grave was destroyed when its branches caught fire in 1841.

A delicately carved statue representing Ann forms part of the lacelike reredos over the altar at Riverside Church in New York City. It is seen by thousands of visitors every year.

ADONIRAM JUDSON

After Ann's death Adoniram remarried, lost his second wife and married a third. He fulfilled his great ambition by completing the Burmese translation of the Bible which is still in use today. His Burmese dictionary was revised a few years ago but is still a standard work. Fate decreed for

242

Adoniram the kind of death Ann always feared for herself —death and burial at sea. He died April 12, 1850.

In 1963 the Christians in Burma will celebrate the one hundred and fiftieth anniversary of the arrival of the Judsons in Burma. The beautiful new church building in the modern downtown city of Rangoon has just been dedicated as a memorial to U Naw (Maung Nau in the old spelling), Adoniram's first Christian convert.

There have been many memorials erected to Adoniram Judson, but no memorial would please him more than the whole Burmese Christian community that now exceeds six hundred thousand in a population of about twenty million people, most of whom are Buddhists. More than two hundred thousand of these Christians are members of the two thousand Baptist churches. They speak thirteen different languages and include not only the Burmese people but many tribal groups.

These Christians support their own churches and ministers, and there are many Christian schools. While American Foreign Missions have given assistance with leadership training and Christian literature, the Christians of Burma have been notable for their self-support and self-direction of their churches, and for their own mission work. They now request missionaries from abroad and assign them to specific tasks. Many of Burma's leaders in civil and business life are Christians.

These churches are members of the World Council of Churches, while their leaders are found on the councils of many world Christian groups.

The "wild romantic undertaking" begun by the young Judsons grew into an enterprising Christian community that has continued without a break since their own day.

243

KING BAGYIDAW

The King became insane and was deposed by the Tharrawaddy Prince in 1837.

DR. JONATHAN PRICE

The rigors of imprisonment left deep scars on the health of Dr. Price. He contracted tuberculosis, which was soon to claim his life. His second (ugly) wife died giving birth to a child.

MAUNG SHWAY-GNONG

The Burmese teacher who was forced to flee from Rangoon for fear of reprisals after he became a Christian died from cholera.

KOO-CHIL, THE BENGALI COOK

He had been brought to Ava from Calcutta by Ann when she returned from her visit to the United States, and he finally became a Christian. He had been particularly devoted to his mistress, keeping her and baby Maria alive during the terrible privations they suffered when Adoniram was incarcerated in the grim Oung-pen-la prison. Of Koo-Chil's conversion Adoniram joyfully writes:

Though a faithful good servant he persisted for years in rejecting all religious instruction, and maintained his allegiance to the false prophet.

But the process was slow, the struggle strong; he felt deeply the responsibility of changing his religion, and when he made his formal request for baptism, he trembled all over. Poor old man! He is above sixty; his cheeks are quite fallen in; his long beard is quite gray; he has probably but a short time to live . . . He affectionately remembers his old mistress, and frequently sheds tears when speaking of the scenes of Ava and Amherst, where he saw her suffer and die.

Koo-Chil had wed a Burmese woman who was baptized in 1834. In 1835 Koo-Chil himself followed her example.

MAH MEN-LAY

The first Burmese woman to be baptized died in September, 1827, full of happy thoughts of meeting her beloved Mrs. "Yoodthan" in heaven. "But first of all," she declared on her deathbed, "I shall hasten to where my Savior sits, and fall down, and worship Him, for His great love in sending the teachers to show me the way to heaven."

When I came to live in the old red brick house near historic Washington Square in New York City's Greenwich Village, the first things that took my fancy were the portraits of the Hasseltine women, especially the one of Ann Hasseltine who married the Reverend Adoniram Judson at Bradford, Massachusetts, in the year 1812.

From the time of Ann's mother, Rebecca Burton Hasseltine, right down to our own generation the Hasseltine women have always been interested in the higher education of their sex. The books Rebecca read by her quiet Bradford fireside laid the foundation that encouraged Ann to accompany Adoniram Judson into the unknown, and another daughter, Abigail, to become preceptress of Bradford Academy. Profiting from Abigail's able leadership, the school, founded in

1803 for both boys and girls under the guiding hand of Abigail's father, Deacon John Hasseltine, and Parson Jonathan Allen, became a pillar of learning in New England. In 1835 the section for boys was discontinued. Today Bradford Academy flourishes as Bradford Junior College.

Another member of the family, Martha Hasseltine Cummings, a great beauty of the Edwardian era, married into the prominent Whitney family. Her drawing rooms held in the Remsen Street mansion on fashionable Brooklyn Heights beckoned the great literary, art- and music-loving minds of the time. She continually fought for the right of women to vote, being among the first in that memorable Woman's Suffrage Parade down New York's Fifth Avenue. Martha's daughter, Isabel Lydia Whitney, a pioneer woman fresco painter in America, has been a great source of information to me while working on this biography of her eminent forebear, Ann Hasseltine Judson. As a point of interest Miss Whitney was recently honored by the American Baptist Foreign Mission Society for having restored for them a large oil portrait of Adoniram Judson painted by George Peter Alexander Healy (1813-1892). Among other notables painted by Healy was President Abraham Lincoln.

My thanks are also due to Pearl S. Buck for her encouragement; the New York Historical Society; V. Isabelle Miller, Curator of Costumes, Furniture and Silver at the Museum of the City of New York; Huldah M. Smith, Acting Director of Essex Institute, Salem, Massachusetts; Hazel F. Shank, Administrative Secretary for Burma and Thailand of the American Baptist Foreign Mission Society, who allowed me to examine and publish personal letters and other informative data pertaining to both Ann and Adoniram Judson, and whose own unfailing interest in my project has been a source of inspiration and encouragement; Mary K. Walker, Librarian to the American Board of Commissioners for Foreign Missions, Boston; the Congregational Library, Boston; Joyce Glover, Antiquarian Bookseller of Eastbourne, England; the staff of the Haverhill Public Library; Edith Gaines, Associate Editor of *Antiques* magazine, for her kindness in helping to to trace a lost portrait of Ann Hasseltine Judson; the Reverend Thomas G. Savins, vicar of Old Heathfield, Sussex, England; Edna Eckert; Gertrude Young; Joseph Anthony Scaltro; Ann Crouch; Salome Bridger, for research done in connection with William Carey; Lillian Watson of Boston, owner of Rembrandt Peale's portrait of Ann; Adeline Emerson Wheeler; Esther R. Stevens; Louise Schooley Hazeltine; Ralph L. Hazeltine; Dale Mitchell, Chairman of the English Department and Historian of the College, Bradford Junior College, Massachusetts; many former students of Bradford Junior College who wrote me concerning the whereabouts of the Peale Portrait of Ann; Dr. Hlu Bu (Professor of Philosophy, retired, Rangoon University) and his wife Daw E. Tin; Mildred Archer of the India Office Library, Commonwealth Relations Office, London, for allowing me to examine Burmese parabaiks (books containing illustrations); the Royal Asiatic Society, London; Tet Htoot, a descendant of King Bagyidaw's most trusted minister; and a host of Burmese friends without whose warm interest this book could not have been written.

New York City.   Gordon Langley Hall

Bibliography

Courtney Anderson—*To The Golden Shore* (The Life of
Adoniram Judson) (Boston, 1956.)

Jonathan Allen—*A Sermon Delivered at Haverhill February
5, 1812, on the Occasion of Two Young Ladies being about
to Embark as the Wives of Rev. Messieurs Judson and
Newell Going Missionaries to India.* (Haverhill, 1812.)

Baptist Missionary Magazine, Boston, 1803-1851. (Known as
Massachusetts Baptist Missionary Magazine, 1803-1817;
American Baptist Magazine, 1817-1836.)

Bradford Academy—*Public Exercises at the Presentation of
the Portraits of Rufus Anderson, D.D., Mrs. Harriet
Newell and Mrs. Ann H. Judson to Bradford Academy,
March 26, 1884.* Included with above.

Circular of Bradford Academy—(Haverhill, Mass., 1884.)

S. Pearce Carey—*William Carey* in two volumes. (London,
1923.)

John L. Christian,—"Americans in the First Anglo-Burmese War" from *Pacific Historical Review,* volume V, pp. 312-314. (Berkeley and Los Angeles, 1936.)

J. Clement—*The Life of the Rev. Adoniram Judson, The Heroic Pioneer Missionary to the Tropics of the Orient, etc.* (Philadelphia, date not given. Published in New York and Auburn, 1857.)

John Crawfurd—*Journal of an Embassy from the Governor General of India to the Court of Ava.* (London, 1829.)

Daniel C. Eddy—*The Three Mrs. Judsons and Other Daughters of the Cross.* (Boston, 1860.)

Burma Crossroads—Prepared for the American Baptist Foreign Mission Society and the Woman's American Baptist Foreign Mission Society by Frederick G. Dickason, Katherine L. Read and Marian Reifsneider. (New York, 1957.)

Henry Gouger—*A Personal Narrative of Two Years' Imprisonment in Burmah.* (London, 1862.)

Phebe A. Hanaford—*Daughters of America* or *Women of the Century.* (Augusta, Maine. My copy has author's dedication date, 1882.)

William Hague—*The Life and Character of Adoniram Judson, Late Missionary to Burma, etc.* (Boston, 1851.)

D.G.E. Hall—*Europe and Burma: A Study of European Relations with Burma to the Annexation of Thibaw's Kingdom in 1886.* (London, 1945.)

Mrs. Ernest Hart—*Picturesque Burma: Past and Present.* (London and Philadelphia, 1897.)

G. E. Harvey—*A History of Burma.* (London, 1925.)

Ethel Daniels Hubbard—*Ann of Ava.* (New York, 1913.)

F. Tennyson Jesse—*The Lacquer Lady.* (London, 1929.)

Adoniram Judson—*The Holy Bible Translated into Burmese.* (Burma, 1840. Many editions and still in active use. Sections published at previous dates as Adoniram completed them.)

English-Burmese Dictionary.

Ann Hasseltine Judson: Contemporary—Four-page leaflet containing reproduction of miniature of Ann painted on ivory about 1811 and discovered in a trunk stored in a Massachusetts attic. (Woman's American Baptist Foreign Mission Society, 1951.)

Ann H. Judson—*An Account of the American Baptist Mission to the Burman Empire, in a Series of Letters Addressed to a Gentleman in London.* (London, 1823.) Also published as *A Particular Relation of the American Baptist Mission to the Burman Empire.* (Washington, 1823.)

Mrs. Judson's Catechism—(Burma, 1817.) Printed in Burmese by George Hough.

R. Talbot Kelly, R.E.A., F.R.G.S.,—*Burma—The Land of the People.* (Boston and Tokyo, 1910.)

James D. Knowles—*Memoir of Mrs. Ann H. Judson, Late Missionary to Burmah, etc.* (Boston, 1829.)

Nelson J. Lewis—*Judson Centennial Services. A Compilation of the Addresses, Papers, and Remarks, Given at These Services* etc. (Malden, 1888.)

Life Magazine—*The World's Great Religions: Buddhism.* (March 7, 1955.)

Basil Miller—*Ann Judson, Heroine of Burma.* (Grand Rapids, Michigan, 1947.)

Eric M. North, Editor—*The Book of a Thousand Tongues: Being Some Account of the Translation and Publication of All or Part of the Holy Scriptures into more than a Thousand Languages and Dialects.* (New York and London, 1938.)

Jean Sarah Pond—*Bradford: A New England Academy.* (Published by the Bradford Alumnae Association, Bradford, Mass., 1930.)

Visitor's Guide to Salem—(Essex Institute, Salem, 1937 and various later editions.)

Herbert Wallace Schneider—*The Puritan Mind.* (New York, 1930.)

A Sermon Delivered at the Tabernacle Church in Salem,

Feb. 6, 1812, on Occasion of the Ordination of the Rev. Messrs. Samuel Newell, A.M., Adoniram Judson, A.M., Samuel Nott, A.M., Gordon Hall, A.M., and Luther Rice, A.B., Missionaries to the Heathen in Asia, etc." (Stockbridge, 1812.)

John E. Skoglund,—*The Spirit Tree.* (Judson Press, Philadelphia, 1951.)

George Smith—*Life of William Carey.* (1885.)

William E. Strong—*The Story of the American Board.* (Boston, 1910.)

Arabella Stuart (Mrs. Arabella M. Willson)—*The Lives of Mrs. Ann H. Judson and Mrs. Sarah B. Judson, with a Biographical Sketch of Mrs. Emily C. Judson, Missionaries to Burma.* (Auburn and Buffalo, 1854.)

Anna Canada Swain—*Ann Hasseltine Judson, Heroine of Ava. From My Book of Missionary Heroines.* (a Sixteen-page pamphlet reprinted by the Baptist Board of Education, New York, 1944.)

Michael Symes, Esq.,—*An Account of an Embassy to the Kingdom of Ava, Sent by the Governor-General of India, in the Year 1795.* (London, 1800. Published in one and three volumes.) My personal copy is a second edition in three volumes.

Stacy R. Warburton—*Eastward! The Story of Adoniram Judson.* (New York, 1937.)

Francis Wayland—*A Memoir of the Life and Labors of the Rev. Adoniram Judson, D.D.* An official biography copyrighted by Judson's third wife, Emily C. Judson. (Boston, 1853.)

Sir Herbert Thirkell White—*Burma.* (Cambridge, 1923.)

Leonard Woods—*A Sermon, Preached at Haverhill, Mass., in Remembrance of Mrs. Harriet Newell, Wife of the Rev. Samuel Newell.* Included also is *Memoirs of Her Life.* (Boston 1814, followed by numerous subsequent editions.)

Walter N. Wyeth—*Ann H. Judson: A Memorial.* (Cincinnati, 1888.)

Shway Yoe, "Subject of the Great Queen,"—*The Burman: His Life and Notions*. (London, 1896.)

Designs of Things in Daily Use in the Golden Palace— Catalogued as Burmese MS. 199. India Office Library, London.